kidjacked
a father's story

a memoir by scott lesnick

•••

JAZZ DOG
PUBLISHING

Praise for *Kidjacked: A Father's Story*

◆ ◆ ◆

"I was so involved in this story I couldn't stop reading it! Scott did such an impeccable job articulating his feelings, thoughts, and the hopelessness he felt that I was in tears too, wondering how I would ever know even the first step to take if I were in the same situation. I truly felt like I was along in this journey; Scott nailed it!!!!!"

ANNALEE KRUGER · PRESIDENT, LBSW, MBA, CGB CARE RIGHT, INC.

"*Kidjacked* is a mesmerizing examination of a seemingly impossible international abduction through a father's eyes. Anyone who's ever faced an insurmountable hurdle will truly be inspired by this story."

CAITLIN O'CONNELL · ATTORNEY

"A compelling story of one father's fight against long odds and even longer miles... a tribute to the determination and faith of a committed parent. Scott Lesnick's clear and concise writing style makes for an easy and pleasurable reading experience."

IRA B. BORDOW · ATTORNEY

"Scott Lesnick shares with us a stark self portrait of his struggle against all odds to recover the most precious gifts he was ever given; his kids."

JIM COLLIS · ATTORNEY

"*Kidjacked* is a love story. It's about a regular guy faced with extraordinary challenges who achieves the impossible. He is tested to his limits and in the process discovers the things that matter most in life... family, friends, perseverance and love. Scott is transformed by his struggle into a stronger, more confident, more compassionate man. Reading his journey reminded me to never give up on the things I believe in. The story is compelling. The message is for everyone."

"One day Scott Lesnick's life dramatically changes when his then wife informs him that she is going to keep their two young children in Israel-permanently. The emotional traumas Scott undergoes and the enormous legal obstacles he must overcome in his efforts to bring them back are not only inspirational, but show how important the dedication of parent is to our society. Anyone who reads this very informative book will not only experience his sense of loss, but gain a new appreciation for the endless efforts a parent will make for the welfare of a child."

kidjacked
a father's story

ISBN: 978-0-9889463-0-9

First Edition

Book Design by AbandonedWest Creative, Inc.

CONTENTS

◆◆◆

	Introduction	9
1	Ultimate Betrayal	11
2	My Man Cliff	37
3	Tough Words	41
4	The Light Bulb Glows Brightly	45
5	The Plot Thickens and the Steel Wall Weakens	51
6	My Plan Takes Shape	57
7	All In	65
8	Israel Bound	67
9	A Bumpy Road	69
10	Is That An Uzi, Ma'am?	77
11	Liza	85
12	Milwaukee 1984	91
13	Come Mary Me, Please	97
14	I've Got Something to Tell You	103
15	Home Again	133
16	The Fight Escalates	161
17	Decision Day	173
18	A New Beginning for the Family	179
19	Meg	183
20	Israel, Again	201
21	David, Shmuel, and Another Battle	207
22	Back In The Lion's Den	221
23	Reunited At Last	229
24	Decision Day	243
25	Oh, Come On!	247
	Epilogue	257
	Final Thoughts	259
	Acknowledgments	263

OCTOBER 29, 1991

◆◆◆

THE DC-10 BEGAN to bank, making its final approach into Ben Gurion International Airport in Tel Aviv, Israel. I felt my pulse and blood pressure rapidly increase as paralyzing thoughts ran through my mind. I sat with my head facing the window, wondering if I had covered all possible angles. Moments of despair made me question if I was simply dreaming of a good outcome or foolishly placing myself in harm's way.

What the hell was I thinking when I decided to do this? Doubting myself while replaying events over and over in my head felt healthy to a point, but I also needed a shot of confidence. I had schemed so long and worked so hard that I would not allow anyone to ruin my element of surprise. I knew I'd have to be one hundred percent convincing or they would see right through me and it would be over quickly. I had no backup plan. I had one week to pull this off. I was going to rescue my son and daughter from the person who kidnapped them—their mother, my wife Liza.

At the time my children were kidnapped, there were no international laws requiring their mother to return them. They were two and four. I was devastated.

She took them to the Middle East—Tiberius, Israel to be exact. I watched helplessly as my life began to unravel. I nearly died when this happened, but I decided to do what I thought would be best for my children: I would locate them and bring them home to Milwaukee, Wisconsin. Of course, it wouldn't be quick and easy. That would be asking too much, and I had so much ahead of me to learn.

I attempted to do what most said couldn't be done. People close to me said to not even try. Others wished me luck. I could read in their faces and hear in the tone of their voices that they had a more realistic view of the probable outcome than I did. "You'll get yourself killed," said more than one friend. "It's very dangerous over there with wars and bombings," said another. "You might have to just move on."

It's true: I had no clue how to proceed, but I also had no choice. There is much to be said about the power of true determination and will. I asked myself, "What am I willing to do now that I'm kid-less? How far am I willing and able to go? How the hell did I allow this to happen in the first place?"

◆ ◆ ◆

CHAPTER 1

ULTIMATE BETRAYAL

◆◆◆

IN EARLY SPRING of 1991, Liza told me that she wanted to take the kids to Israel for two months during the summer. My first response had to do with money, because tickets were expensive. I went on to say that I would miss them a lot as I had envisioned a different life with my wife and children, not one that kept us apart for weeks and months at a time. Sitting at our kitchen sipping my morning coffee, I explained that the cost of flying, which came in at $2,400, and keeping my job were two big concerns. Standing with her own cup and peering out our bay window, she didn't appear bothered. Getting what she wanted, Liza remained focused on one thing: two children and tickets home to see her family. "If you can't come then it is okay, because I will have plenty of help. Besides, we need food and a house and you can make more money if you stay and work."

As I had done every year since we were married, I acquiesced. Thrilled, Liza said that I would have to come and visit so that we could all be together as a family.

My job continued to be challenging, though I did well and had become a bit of a selling machine. I hated the idea of being separated as a family, yet I knew this would make my wife happy. Happy wife equals happy life and husband, so the saying goes. Liza made the flight plans the very next day. Early in June, we packed up the car and the four of us drove the 90 miles from Milwaukee to Chicago's O'Hare International Airport. They flew out and landed safely in Tel Aviv.

The first week I tried to get into a rhythm, reminding myself that I had to provide for my family and pay our bills. Since they all shared birthdays in June close to each other I called on June 18, to wish Jonathan a happy birthday. After I talked to him and said a few words to Ally, Liza got back on the phone. "Scotty, I just wanted to tell you that I am staying here with the kids in Israel and we are not coming back. I'm sorry, but I want to be in here and I told you this... Are you still there?"

This was an instant shocker, as well as a loss of most of the air in my lungs. Literally without words for a few seconds, I finally blurted out, "What do you mean?"

"The kids need to be raised in Israel and America is not their home. I don't want to live there anymore."

"Well, I thought it was! After all, we are raising them here." I had to ask the question, dreading the answer. "Are you kidding me, Liza? This is serious and these are *our* children, not only yours to play games with."

"No, Scott, I am not joking. I have made up my mind. You'll have to move on without us." So cold in her tone and in an uncharacteristically calm voice, Liza continued to explain how she needed to be near her family and with her kids. I noticed that she began to call them *her* kids, not ours.

The change had already begun from our children to hers? She stated that whether I came to live there or not, she and the children were not flying back. I could hear the tenseness as her voice began to tremble, yet she remained safe in her parents' home in the hills of Tiberius, surrounded by loved ones.

I begged and pleaded, immediately realizing that the children and I were in deep trouble, but to no avail. "Please, Liza. You can't do this to us. You can't do this to our children. It will hurt them so much!" I yelled.

"I don't care anymore and you are going to have to understand, Scott. My life is here. We are here and I will never come back there," she said coldly.

Pacing back and forth holding the phone in a death grip, I broke into a cold sweat. My right hand flailing in the air to help accentuate my disapproval made me look like a conductor at the symphony. Her mind was made up; there would be no reasoning with Liza. When I inquired as to what was to become of me, she harshly said that I could remarry and have more children. She said, "My time is running out. I want more kids and I want to have them here."

Apparently, she felt that she was doing a great job as a parent. Now completely beside myself, I ended the conversation abruptly after being told to move on with my life. Slamming down the phone, I began to pace around our house. "You've got to be kidding me. You've got to be kidding me. Shit! This can't be happening to me," I chanted slapping my face to make sure it wasn't simply a horrible dream.

So many thoughts raced around in my head. I wondered if I could find a quick fix to the situation. Could I possibly figure this out and have a now-defiant wife hop back on a plane to the U.S. with our kids in tow?

I thought, I'll fly over there and get them. I'll call and ask her to reconsider, reminding her that I am their father. I'll explain that our income is coming from my job in the States and our financial security depends on us living in Milwaukee. I could beg, grovel, and beg some more and try to reason with her, working on her sympathy. I could speak with her father, her mother, brothers and sisters. Shaking my head, I yelled what-ever came to mind and freaked out walking around our house like a lunatic.

No compassion was forthcoming from Liza, and so began my chaotic search for a solution to an impossible situation. Later that night, I laid my head on my pillow and closed my eyes. This meant the end of us, I realized, and most likely there would be a messy divorce. I cried.

My dreams were fractured as I woke up alone the following morning to a cloudy day.

My kids were gone and the one I trusted the most and shared my bed with every night had taken them. Each evening I'd lie on the floor between their bedrooms and read to them. They'd giggle and sometimes ask for more stories. I always found the energy to read a few more no matter how tired I was. Those were magical moments.

While I entertained our kids, Liza would sip vodka and smoke a few cigarettes outside. Many nights we'd sit in the den and discuss her desire to move back to Israel. Now that we had two kids, her drive to get me to move felt unrelenting. We both agreed there were limited opportunities for work in Israel, but that didn't stop her. The person I once met while on vacation at the bottom of her small country, who claimed to be an independent woman, no longer wanted to live in America.

Now all alone, it would be quite a while before I had a viable plan, not to mention the heightened sense of courage needed to get on a jet to Israel. I realized the horrible position I was in as I struggled to keep it together. I felt as though I had been shot in the chest twice and could hear my heart pounding as I neared life support. Blindsided and left with no power or logical next move to bring a quick resolution to my horrific circumstances, I cried again and then grew angry. I pounded my fists against my chest like a gorilla and banged on walls to relieve some stress. Then I tried to cut myself some slack. After all, I figured, we've all heard people in crisis situations stating that their whole world lay crumbling around them. This described me well utterly alone and helpless. I needed to be with my kids, loved them with all my heart, and this deep-seated paternal instinct helped keep me focused.

Arriving home after work I'd walk aimlessly through different rooms in my house looking at pictures of the four of us. Many thoughts regarding the lengths I'd go to see to my children's safe return began rushing through my head. I would do anything, I reasoned, just to get them back with me. But reality can get in the way of desire, as I discovered so often during my five-month journey to reunite with my children. I lay on our brown leather couch, my feet stretched out. Shaking my head, I convinced myself that reckless behavior like kidnapping was usually perpetrated by men. I soon discovered that women *kidjack* their children quite often as well. I never imagined this fate would one day become my reality. I shouted at the living room walls, "I'll be a better person in every way if I can just be with my kids again. What's happening here? What on earth am I supposed to do? What the hell am I suppose to do?" I sat up, feeling awful, left holding only a picture of my children.

I continued trying to process what had occurred. I'd seen this on TV and read about it in the newspaper. This happens to other people, not me. Women only did this if they or the children were in imminent harm, I reasoned. There was zero danger staring Liza in the face and no fear in our home. We lived in a charming English Tudor with lead-trimmed windows on a tree-lined street five blocks from the lake. The neighborhood was safe and desirable. She simply wanted things her way with no regard for anyone else, including our children. A desperate longing to be home, surrounded by her large family, pulled hard at her core.

I thought my wife would always put the best interests of our children first. Proven wrong, I paid a heavy price. I flashed back to conversations as Liza would dismiss the white lies she often told, explaining, "It's no big deal, everyone does that."

As I began to further scrutinize our relationship, I realized that signs were there if I had looked closer, but I simply never saw this one coming. I sat at our kitchen table, shocked, and left with a fractured and weak foundation that no longer provided the support necessary to maintain our marriage.

Numb in mind and body, sometimes feeling too weak to eat, run, or talk to people. I began to privately crawl into a safe and protective shell, allowing few in, and so began my unwanted journey.

I couldn't think clearly because my brain constantly raced. Tears flowed. Nighttime proved to be the worst for me. Eerily quiet, I walked from room to room searching for something, anything to help lift my spirits and point me in the right direction. The saving grace, I suppose, was that I felt so exhausted by 9 p.m. that not sleeping was rarely an issue.

I'd awake in the morning to a brief period of temporary amnesia. As my feet hit the floor, I'd sit on the edge of the bed trying to muster up the courage to stand and go about my day. But first, my mind always checked in with our children and what signs I missed.

At night after reading to our kids and tucking them in bed I made my way downstairs. One week before they'd be leaving, Liza and I sat at outside on our patio admiring the abundant stars and eating fruit from a bowl we received at our wedding. She never mentioned a thing about Israel. Instead, she smiled as I entertained her with stories about Ally trying to hide under her blanket until I found her.

We laughed uncontrollably and had to cover our mouths so our light sleepers wouldn't hear us through their open windows and wake up. "Yes Liza, that noise you heard was my big left toe slamming against the bedroom door as I flew each of them up high like an airplane. Yes, Jonathan thought it was hilarious as he and his sister giggled forever, but I finally got them to go to sleep."

My mind would go back to our fearless daughter with her adorable red curls. Ally loved climbing on my shoulders and head while I stood in our living room. She'd encouraged me to let her try and balance. Her laugh was as contagious as her brother's and she had such a sweet disposition. Jonathan would always get into something. I loved his curiosity. He continued to be the King of Questions and did not simply want an answer; he wanted to understand. Always on the move or getting into something usually harmless, "Action" was my nickname for him, although his other nickname was Yoni (Johnny in Hebrew).

I'd get off my bed, head to the bathroom and remind myself every morning that I had to stay strong and focused for their sake. Some days I'd yell and others I'd cry, but every day I made myself move about the city, do what I had to do, and not shut down.

I drove from account to account doing my best to keep up appearances while wondering what they were doing right now. Were they safe and happy? Did they miss me as much as I missed them? Did they know what was happening? How did Liza explain my absence and lack of contact to our children? I realized she didn't tell them the truth, but how much did she lie to cover her actions?

I'd enter haze-like moments of the four of us in flashbacks. Only weeks before, we had gone on a picnic by a beautiful lake an hour from our home. Ally ran around, falling down on the grass and getting back up. We'd tossed a small ball at her feet and applauded for joy at her attempts to send it back in our direction. She'd follow her brother and watch as he tried to skip stones in the water. Jonathan tested his boundaries by sticking his feet in the warm water with his sandals on. I'd walked over to help him take them off. He'd run back to get them, quickly trying to put them on as he staggered toward the water, hoping that I'd chase after him.

We let them make the sandwiches from the food we brought and laughed loudly at the size of the feast they prepared, knowing that we'd never be able to open our mouths wide enough to fit around the bread.

Now in Milwaukee alone, my daily activities began to blur.

The first few weeks were painful as I moved sloth-like about the city. I focused intensely on two points of light in the far distance that I missed and loved dearly.

I felt my body shutting down and my mind weak from so much thought. I would call friends to vent and my best friend, Bobby, although it was difficult for him to fully comprehend, could always make me laugh. "Buddy," he'd say, "everything is going to turn out fine. If it doesn't, you can always come live with us for a slight fee."

Staring out our kitchen window and watching the birds eat the food I'd put out that morning, I'd remind him of my empty house and all the room I had. Joking, he said "OK fine, I'll stay with you on the weekends. Hey, how are you progressing? Have you come up with any plan of attack to bring them back? Should we go get them on our own, Buddy? I'll do it I swear."

"I haven't got squat yet," I said. "But I'll come up with something. I have to, for their sake."

"Isn't there someone that you can call? This is a government issue, right? Let's call a senator and get them to help you."

With two fingers barely holding the phone on my left shoulder and a face that looked like it had just heard a bad joke, I replied, "I'm working on it."

I said goodbye and sat quietly with my eyes closed doing deep breathing exercises.

This crisis took me to a place I'd never been before. So profoundly personal, my children's lives now hung delicately between America and Israel.

I knew that I had to push myself hard to continue moving forward. I had to build on thoughts and ideas, however small that would creep into my head.

I searched hard to come up with a plan to bring my children home. It was 1991, and I had no Internet to scour, so I spent most evenings walking back and forth to the library until it closed. Precious few articles and books were available, but I continued my search for any morsel of solid information that might help. I realized it might get dirty, and rules, perhaps laws, might be bent or broken to assure their safe return. I was fine with that.

My attitude and focus remained fueled with the simple belief that the children and I were being wronged. I sat at the dining room table with a single light shining on all my papers anxiously trying to develop three or four plans to rescue them like they do in the movies, but I didn't care for the downside. No matter that the cost in dollars was more than I had. I thought, you have to look at *all* options before saying no to any of them. While I continued to play possible scenarios in my mind, the following cynical thoughts kept popping up: 1. This is the Mideast, you idiot. Who do you think you are, Rambo? 2. This is Israel, you dummy. They're prepared for massive attacks, but you'll be able to walk in, get the kids, and walk out, no problem, 3. A lifetime of jail far from home would be horrible, and 4. I could get killed.

How could this help the children? I kept plotting. Exhausted at the end of every day, I would plop down on the floor in our den and lie on my back staring at the ceiling. I schemed continuously, putting up a calm front while physically torn up on the inside, yelling at myself if I felt I was being too wimpy or weak. "Come on, man. You need to stay strong and focused for the kids. Don't let them down. This is their entire lives we're talking about. Keep your shit together, Scott."

Three weeks had passed since Liza told me she was staying in Israel with our children. Because of the eight hour time difference I waited until midnight before picking up the phone to once again try and contact her. One of her brothers answered and appeared distant. He told me that she had left with the kids to visit her sister in Tel Aviv. Not surprisingly, when I called her sister, she sternly told me that they were not there and hung up the phone. Why didn't they tell their sister the huge mistake she was making and how the best interests of our children were surely being overlooked?

I struggled to have a positive attitude moving forward when I might have otherwise abandoned ship, or worse, gone down with it.

A constant mental battle played over and over in my heart and mind, but I worked and I smiled and I ran and I cried. During the day as I worked, I'd observe people going about their daily lives with what appeared to be not a care in the world. I'd notice husbands holding hands with their wives, girls talking to boys, and children everywhere. I envied them.

I was working for a large carpet manufacturer as a representative, and thankfully things were going well. I kept my sales strong, because I was going to need the income. I was walking wounded, but my job helped in several ways. It allowed me to focus on something else while also providing money and the ability to plan. It also helped me maintain some much needed balance during these complex times. I drove to stores around southeastern Wisconsin selling carpet, and thankfully I could take personal time whenever I needed. Bob, my manager at work, was my mentor in the floor-covering industry. He continued to be supportive of my plight. 12 years my senior, he had a much-needed perspective and a brown beard that added a dash of wisdom.

"Scotty, you just do whatever you need to do to get those kids home. I've got your back."

"I don't know how or what to do, Bob. This is bigger than me and I've never experienced anything like it. I'm frightened for the kids, man. I don't have a clue as to what is happening with them. I can't talk to them and I'm not exactly sure where they're living. This really sucks!"

"Get a good lawyer or hire someone to bring them to you. Do you know anyone over there that could assist you? Don't you dare give up, partner. Your children need a father!"

"I'm thinking about all my options every waking moment Bob, but I don't have a solid direction yet and I don't have anyone over there I can call."

"What about people here? Someone must know what to do. This is ridiculous. Can ya get the government involved?"

"Good thought. I'm going to turn over every stone I can until I get the answers that will help me bring them back to Milwaukee."

Bob helped me plot strategies while trying to lift my spirits with his raunchy sense of humor. I was grateful as well as lucky to have him alongside me during these tumultuous times. A good person to have when going into battle, because he was street-wise and bully-tested. Growing up on the south side of Chicago, Bob had experience and street-savvy that I didn't, and he knew our kids. He cared, and he encouraged me to stay strong and get tougher while always reminding me to watch my back.

A daily head game played out before me. I'd wake in the morning to an empty house. I spent most of my days angry, determined, frightened, sad and lonely. Unsure of myself, I constantly questioned whether I was going about the return of Jonathan and Alexandra in the best way possible.

I'd walk into my home office. The floor, littered with crumpled sheets of paper, showed plenty of effort, but no solutions. I'd flip my pen in the air, trying to catch it between my index and middle finger to reduce stress. I figured there'd be possibly one opportunity to bring my children home, if I was lucky.

Internally, extreme checks and balances were constantly occurring. I developed strategies, while tossing out ideas that my mind and gut said were not going to work. I tossed out a lot.

You've got one shot to make this work, Scott, I kept reminding myself. One shot! The problem for me remained my lack of direction with which to take aim and shoot. I called my older sister Carole for direction.

She was passionate about my plight and furious with Liza. "I can't believe a mother would do this to her own children, Scotty!"

I let her vent until she got it all out. "So what have you got for me, big sister? Are you going to save the day like you used to when we were young?"

"Scotty, I think you are in big trouble here. People I've spoken to are outraged by Liza's behavior, but there were no suggestions good enough to pass on to you. Can't you have her arrested?"

"I don't know. I'm at a loss, as well, and damn angry. It's been over three weeks since they left."

Carole said, "Sometimes when I visited, Liza told me that the children were her entire life. She said she'd die without them. I had asked her, 'what did you do your whole life before the kids?'

"'I did what I wanted to do until I met Scotty. Then, I knew I needed to get married and be a mother. I want to travel around the world with them and live like a gypsy. I wanted to live in America. Is that bad?'" Liza had confided.

"'How would you pay for this?'" Carole had asked her.

"'Now Scotty has a good job and we are doing fine. It's a good thing I can't find work because I like being home.'"

Carole also said that she could sense something during her last visit, but she couldn't put her finger on it at first. We talked a bit more and she added, "I'm worried for your safety. Liza is capable of anything. Are you planning on going to Israel?"

Now pacing back and forth in the kitchen I replied, "I've thought about it, but what could I do there? I would be alone in the Mideast with no protection from our government except the Embassy as a safe haven. It's a long way to go with no plan. Bobby and I discussed this as well and didn't come up with any concrete ideas."

We promised to stay in touch as we said our goodbyes.

I knew that a two- and a four-year-old were gone from my life in a day. I realized that ours was not a perfect marriage, but kidnapping our children had never entered my mind. Why would it? I now realized that Liza must have been planning this for a while.

No inner filter when speaking, lying when she felt the need, and always believing she was right should have tipped me off. I smiled momentarily, remembering some of her antics and abnormal behavior, along with her energy.

My mind quickly went back to her lying. The lies had continued, and she dismissed them as meaningless "white lies," as if they didn't hold the same power as a *real lie.*

One day, months before she took our children, I received a call from Bobby's wife, Sandy. A mother herself, she was beside herself. "Scotty, I have to tell you what Liza has been doing. She dropped Jonathan off at our home on several occasions without calling. She asked me to watch him and not give him any food, only water. When I asked her why, she stated that she didn't want him to get fat. Can you believe that? He's only three."

I thanked Sandy for telling me. "Where has she been going?"

"I'm not sure," she said. "But I felt awful."

She continued: "Liza is not spending much time with them when you're at work. I know this because others have told me that she tries to get them to watch the children, too."

"Thanks for letting me know this," I said in bewilderment. As I hung up the phone I began to think about all the friends I had. I began to notice a pattern developing about six months after our marriage. I was hearing from them less and less, as if I were being ostracized. I later found out that people were pushing away from Liza, not me. I headed outside to walk to the lake as a gentle rain began to fall. My mind racing so quickly I could barely keep up.

One evening when the kids were sleeping, I confronted Liza about the claim Sandy had made, and she assured me that it had happened only once. Hoping for plausible deniability and believing I'd drop the issue, Liza walked away, but I decided to open it up further by talking to other mothers and friends who validated what Sandy had told me.

Dishonesty and fading trust forced me to ask myself why I chose to marry her. I felt so alive when we met and believed we were happy together, but the reality of my distorted marriage became clear.

I turned for home as the rain increased in intensity. I knew where our relationship was heading and I was sick about it. I wondered if she felt the same.

Early in our marriage, Liza and I would have talks late at night. We'd laugh about the kids' antics. She wanted a lot from life, but had no concrete plans on how she would make it happen.

I walked inside my house soaked from head to toe. I took off my shoes, wrung out my socks in the basement sink and changed into some dry clothes.

I was desperate and lost, and although I moved forward a bit most days, I never thought about moving on.

My desperation and anger, coupled with my imagination, took me places I'd never been before. Perhaps I could woo her back with love letters and flowers. Maybe she'll see the error in her ways and come home next week. I could have her come up "missing" and get the kids back.

Suggestions on how I might see the safe return of my children were many. I listened to all of them in hopes of hearing the right words to propel me toward their safe return. "Hire some mercenaries to get her back," said a lady who watched too much TV. "Have you ever thought of moving to Israel?" another person suggested. "Try to reason with her. She'll probably come around."

At work, with friends and acquaintances I found myself opening up more with regard to my personal life and even embraced doing so. This was good for me and proved to be less expensive than seeing a shrink every day.

I was embarrassed and ashamed and felt guilty for allowing this to happen. I would stand weak and limp with my head hanging as I would tell my story to anyone I thought might have an answer. I felt I had failed my kids by not seeing this and stopping it before it happened.

At night, I continued pacing from room to room in my empty house like a caged animal. "What the hell am I supposed to do?" I wondered. I continued to call Israel but had little luck speaking with Liza or our children.

I was working with a seven to eight hour time difference, depending on the time of year, and I was denied access for reasons still unknown today. I sent letters but sadly did not receive a reply.

Four weeks had passed in a matter of minutes and I was no closer than when I originally received the horrible news. When I was finally able to talk to Liza after almost five weeks, she told me that she was fed up with her life in the U.S. and just wanted to be home. "I have no life there, Scott. What do you want me to do? I've tried, and I miss my family. There's nothing for me in Milwaukee. You'll be fine. Just let us be. I'm very busy here."

"Do you actually think I'm going to just sit back and allow you to take our children from my life without a fight?" I asked.

Eating pistachios loudly into the phone and sounding confident to the point of cocky, she replied, "Yeah, you can do what you want. I need to be with them more than you do, Scott, and I will raise them to be good people. I think this is best for everyone."

"Will you raise our daughter and son to leave their spouse with their children because they feel like it?" I yelled.

Had I not been so serious, it might have sounded like a grade school argument, though I was terrified with every word that left my mouth. Liza was aware of the physical distance between us, and I was beginning to realize more than ever that compromise and rational thought were not part of her makeup.

Nestled comfortably in the hills of Tiberius in a modest home surrounded by aged trees and a large family, Liza was in control and acted the part. "I don't want to talk to you anymore, Scott! Just leave us be and I will tell the kids that they have a great father. If ya don't than I..."

I was stunned by this and said the only thing I could think of: "Liza, they do have a great father; it's their mother that's broken!"

She hung up the phone.

Life in America was not as she imagined for herself and her kids, so the small-town girl with curls below her shoulders slipped back to the historic hills of Tiberius. I could hardly understand how this self-proclaimed independent woman missed her mother and father so much that she moved in with them. She told me calmly that I could move to Tiberius and get a job. "You'll be fine here and you can see the kids from time to time when I'm busy."

I knew that would never happen. As for work in Israel, newspapers and magazines inside the U.S. and outside as well were reporting that people were leaving Israel *en masse* to find a better life for themselves and their families.

Sadly, I had to entertain her offer, since it allowed me the opportunity to be with my children, and I listened to all ideas and possibilities. I also realized that I could never trust her, but I wasn't about to tell her that. Oh, I wanted to tell her many things while going off on a two-hour rant to her about how she had hurt our family. I had to remember that *all* ideas were on the table; they simply weren't acted upon for various reasons.

Looking back, this crucial move on my part was the correct one because Liza had no reason not to trust me. I realized that the kids and I were in deep trouble and left with few options. I could almost give Liza credit for pulling this off, but knowing her, I realized that she could never have planned and executed it so well on her own. She had help along the way. I didn't care who; only my children's well-being mattered.

As I plunged deeper into the morass, I began to realize that another large obstacle blocked my way. Even though I tried with all my might, it proved too heavy to budge. So big in fact, that even our government could not help. When I tried to solicit help from the State Department, they told me that at the time of their kidnapping, the U.S. and Israel did not have an agreement with regard to the extradition of minors. It is a document called The Hague Treaty or The Hague Convention. The Convention on the Civil Aspects of International Child Abduction took place on October 25, 1980. Israel had not yet become a signatory to this document, unlike many other countries. In essence, you could take a child from the United States to Israel to live without the permission of the other parent. As unbelievable as it sounds, a parent with Israeli citizenship could, without fear of prosecution, take children away from the other parent and nothing could be done. You've got to be kidding me. All the money we give them and they never signed this piece of paper!

Despair and contempt coursed through me. Why did our politicians allow this to occur? Are we not supposed to be protected by our government? I assumed that all of the legal barriers to protect us from this and other devastating experiences were in place as we go about our daily lives. Our countries were supposed to be "friends." What the hell could I do? My own government was unable or unwilling to bring them home. My letters to U.S. officials did not help.

After exhausting my calls to the State Department and local and state officials and being placed on perpetual hold, I realized that my direction had to change. They did, however, advise me to contact a lawyer. The sad bit of reality hit me as I realized my children and I were not important enough to rate special help. I remember telling more than one official, "If these were their children, I bet they would have made those back room phone calls and had them home in a matter of days."

My emotions were conflicted. Besides being angry, very angry, I had intense feelings of hopelessness, helplessness, and self-pity. I needed to channel this anger; it desperately needed an outlet. Thankfully, I'm a runner. The benefits are many, and I began to run more and started to take out my aggression on the heavy punching bag at my club. This helped some, and my anger levels stayed in check most of the time and my repeated attempts to *take it down* always fell short.

As my crisis continued, I began to think more rationally, giving way to my feelings and emotions as they came. I watched with curiosity as I began changing before my eyes and adapting, as best I could, during these periods of intense stress. Once again, anger would set in and I'd have to admit to myself that I was no one in the eyes of those with power and connections.

Local and state officials suggested I contact the Israeli consulate, which I promptly did. They were no help either, and my gut told me after speaking with them several times that they would rather have our children in Israel. I can't prove this, but they didn't seem concerned with my plight. "I'm sorry, but there is nothing we can do for you," they'd respond in an impartial or reserved manner. "Have you tried calling their mother?"

They reminded me that because their mother was Israeli, our children had Israeli citizenship as well. People who had no stake in my life, or in the kids', for that matter, were telling me what could not be done. I would call on different days and try to speak with different people. I wrote down their names. I called Chicago, New York, London and the Israeli Consulate in Jerusalem, but all of the men and women had the same answer. Oh, I became more than just surprised and lost; I began building up a healthy case of "screw you's," which had the added positive side effect of pushing me harder.

I called the local bar association in Milwaukee and they, too, had no clue as to what my next move would be. Politely they told me that they were a referral association and could not give out any legal advice.

Gesturing with my arms as if they were in the same room, I pleaded. I'd take any advice they could think of. In the end, they offered me a few names of attorneys who might know something about divorce law. Another path appeared and I took it with eyes wide open and a dash of hope. I called the attorneys. They each told me that according to the law, I could not make her return the children. Placing the phone down, I shook my head again thinking, "Shit, I am their father and I can't make her return our children!"

These were top-notch lawyers, and I stumped each one of them when I asked what they might do if it were their children; a fact I am not proud of, but they did give it to me straight. I asked if there wasn't some avenue I could go down to help retrieve them. They offered nothing except that I should be careful, and they wished me good luck. No apparent signs were showing me the right course of action, yet I believed that if I continued to move forward, however slightly, I would get a break at some point, as I would not entertain the notion of quitting.

Back at the library, I tried to uncover articles or books that might offer a gem of an idea or point me in another direction. Late one evening as I sifted through magazines a weird thought came to me. I realized one important advantage I had, the luxury of time, though it was desperate and debilitating, as I longed to be with Yoni and Ally. I didn't have to get the kids home tomorrow, though I'd love it if I could. Liza had no plans of returning them, so every day she kept them boded well for her, as our children were supposedly close by her side. She would not allow me to speak with the kids and her family kept me from contacting her after she hung up the phone on me.

I'd thought about times at home with the four of us and some of the things she said. One evening after I put the kids to bed, I came downstairs to find Liza yelling at one of my friends on the phone. I interrupted to ask her why she was screaming and she replied, "Nobody understands how hard it is to be a mother and a wife, Scotty."

"OK. What is really going on here?" I asked.

"It's so hard doing this and I feel like I'm the only one who gets it. Other women I talk to tell me I'm too selfish, but I think they are jealous of the life I have. Ya know what I mean? I think I am too smart and people are always disagreeing with me. Scott, I love your friends, but I don't think they feel the same way."

Another time when we were bathing the children she blurted out, "I've never seen children so in love with their mother. They would die without me. It's like I am their oxygen."

No internal filter and little respect for their dad made me wonder what I had gotten myself into. Looking back, I realized that she had never really grown up. A childlike woman had full control over our children now, and I'd have to go through her or around her. At one time I felt close with her family. I believed they loved me, as I did them, but they took her side without ever attempting to contact me.

Seven weeks had passed since Yoni and Ally had been kidjacked and I used every day from morning to night to work on their safe return. Their tickets back home to the States were probably sitting in some drawer, along with their passports, and the return date had come and gone. I knew that Liza didn't hate me; in fact, I had a hunch that she probably still loved me. She just had an enormous desire to live in Israel with our kids and was making the calculated mistake of her life.

I now had the element of surprise, as well as time to figure out what plan I could devise. I presumed her family didn't know about The Hague Treaty or the burning hole in my heart. Did they think about me or the terrible effect this would have on the little ones? Did they care about the children's father or the future of our family? As I saw it, no calls to me meant they were now the enemy and not to be trusted.

The following morning I looked through the phone book for attorneys and began making calls to family law practitioners. I called fifteen of them. Most had little to offer, but a few were kind enough to speak with me on the phone. They told me that if I were able to see to the safe return of my children, they'd be happy to represent me in court. That would be fine by me, but I needed a coach and a player like Peyton Manning who could score during the last two minutes of a football game, not a "bring 'em home and we'll help" offer.

After a few days of speaking with attorneys and rabbis, I realized how hopeless the situation was. Two of Milwaukee's finest lawyers told me, "I am sorry. I do not know what you can do."

I pleaded to one rabbi, "Don't you have some connections over there? Is there no one you can think of that might be able to assist me?"

Again, I continued to open up to complete strangers in desperation, only to be told that they had no idea how I should proceed. Even Milwaukee's head rabbi told me that he would not be able to help.

My sister Carole had come to town from Los Angeles to help me sort things out and saw the rabbi with me.

We sat and drank tea in his dark study overflowing with books. The one window let in some welcome light. His long grey beard and black clothing offered a bit of mysticism to our conversation. Carole liked him but grew concerned, as did I, that he had no concrete ideas for us. We asked if he had any contacts in Israel that could help us but he said that he did not.

We thanked him and his wife for their time and left his busy home no wiser than when we arrived. Sitting outside at a café eating lunch under blue skies, Carole asked, "Do you think that you can even get the kids to listen to you after Liza is done brainwashing them? Things are not good here, Scotty and I'm worried sick for you and the kids. What if you get them home somehow and they are all messed up?"

"I hate that last question, but I love ya for asking it, sis. The truth is that I know very little about the long-range effect that their mother's mind control will have on them. Anything is possible, and I plan on dealing with this, and other issues, right here at home when I fly back with them."

"So how do you think that you will be able to do that? I'm worried you'll get hurt. I know you'll never give up and that's great, but how in hell are you going to get my niece and nephew back?"

"I'm not sure, but I don't envision the three of them hopping a plane and landing in the States."

Carole just looked at me with tears running down her cheeks, smiled gently, and gave me a big hug. Always wanting to help and protect her little brother, she too appeared worried and at a loss, and her solemn face showed it.

The next day we talk over dinner at a downtown pizza joint, sharing bottle of wine. I gained a clearer vision, and her outrage and anger continued to refuel me. The following day she headed back to L.A.

Eight weeks had passed now and only my family and a few close friends were staying in touch on a regular basis. It's like the death of a loved one. You are on your own after some time. People were going about their lives, and I continued going about mine the best I could.

Then, I got my first big break.

◆ ◆ ◆

CHAPTER 2

MY MAN CLIFF

◆◆◆

ONE ATTORNEY NAMED Cliff did call me back and offered some
hope. He graciously invited me to visit him in his office. An
enormous break, because I had finally found someone familiar
with family law who agreed to sit down with me (for more than
fifteen minutes).

In his day, Cliff was a top-notch attorney with huge victories
to his credit. He had represented some of the biggest names in
the state. About sixty-five years old, he had many connections
and took an interest in my plight. A chain-smoking, slender
man (whose worn and wrinkled face showed his addiction to
nicotine) also packed a raw sense of humor and a razor-sharp
mind, Cliff took me under his wing and appeared to be the
calmest and most professional person I'd ever met. We sat in
his smoke-filled, modestly decorated office at a big table, and he
puffed away while we discussed my seemingly limited options.
He, too, had trouble with an ex-wife, so the sympathetic Cliff
appeared, and I welcomed him. He wanted no money. He freely

gave his time and experience for no other reason than he wanted to help guide me.

He sat before me with a wealth of legal knowledge and a willingness to share it with me. Although winding down an illustrious career, he still had some fight in him and a keen understanding of the legal system. Perhaps the best things were his creativity and his willingness to say absolutely anything. Thrilled to have his counsel and experience to help me through this colossal mess, I listened to every word.

I learned that he was a bit of a softy for the underdog. Children were innocent to him and they offered up more honesty and integrity than the professional world he had been a part of for four decades. He shared with me that, because of events from his personal life and some challenging cases he took on over the years, he liked a fight that championed a worthy cause. We had six meetings in all, mulling over various ways to get my kids home. "I know that she's a tough and stubborn Israeli, but you are their father," he said. "You have three choices, kid. You can let them go and move on, which I don't really like. You can hire someone to try and retrieve them, or you can schmooze the hell out of her and get her ass back to America with your children where they belong."

"I tried schmoozing her, Cliff. I have had no luck and she holds all of the cards right now. If I were in the same room it might make a difference. Hell, I don't know."

"You could hire someone to help bring them back, but it would be expensive and risky."

"What am I supposed to do here? Call 1-800-Get-My-Kids-Back or something? I don't know anyone like that, do you?"

Gently nodding without saying a word, I knew he understood

my predicament. "Do you have any family over there that could talk with her—you know, try to reason with Liza?"

"I only know *her* family and they've made it clear whose side they're on, and it's not mine."

Cliff sat in his chair blowing smoke rings while staring off into space and remained silent for several minutes. I began to get comfortable with this no-talking approach and found myself gazing at the smoky-blue haze that filled his large office. I could almost hear the wheels turning in his mind as he planted his gaze on me, blinking occasionally.

Finally, he spoke, "Well kid, if you want your children back, I think you're going to have to go get 'em yourself. No government official is going to put their ass on the line for you. Sorry. They don't give a crap about you and you have nothing they want."

Looking up from my yellow legal pad I said, "Yeah? Well how am I supposed to do that, Cliff? I have no special ops training and most everyone over there has served in the military." Nodding and smiling out of the left side of his mouth I continued. "There are a lot of guns Cliff, a lot! I don't care for those odds. There's got to be another way, right?"

Walking around the large conference table I confessed, "I'm in trouble, Cliff, and so are the kids if Liza hangs on to them!"

"Then go get them," he said. "I don't know how, but that's what you have to do. No one else can do this but you, Scott."

My eyes widened. "Are you talking about crossing borders with no passports in the Middle East? I don't see that ending up well. I've got to stay out of prison if I'm going to raise these little ones."

"Right, so then that leaves you with one less option. I'd go with you but I'm getting too old to chase around the world."

Eating a sandwich I brought in for lunch he exclaimed, "Don't you dare give up on your children, they need you!"

I listened carefully to his words, extended my arms for a hug, and said thank you and good-bye to Cliff. I knew what I needed to do. He reopened my mind to continuing the "soft" approach. I would focus all of my efforts into trying to break down Liza's impenetrable steel wall.

My brain required cleansing so that I could continue to work on a plan. I decided to seek the help of a professional who was talented, kind, and brutally honest.

◆ ◆ ◆

CHAPTER 3
TOUGH WORDS

◆◆◆

I HAD CALLED every person I could think of and they, too, were stumped. I delved into my personal life with total strangers. The experience proved to be profoundly humbling and quite an awakening.

As the days crawled on, I decided to see a therapist named John. A bit stocky, he had little hair and a nicely trimmed grey beard, a sharp mind and deep laugh. I felt comfortable and knew that I could learn from his twenty-five years of practice. Like all new forms of exercise, this one took effort and time before results occurred. After working on it, I could feel that something good was happening, which helped lift me up during a dark period in my life.

His office had colorful paintings and art objects that were pleasing to the eyes. I'd find myself gazing at one of his nicely framed pictures or pieces while we spoke, never missing a word he said.

At one point during my third session, I sat in a chair across from him, listening as he told me that he didn't think I would be able to get the kids home. "Young man, you are going to attempt something that has little chance of succeeding. It may be best not to get your hopes up too much, as you could be in for a terrible fall. The simple fact, appalling as it might be, is that she can stay put forever and you have little say in that."

"Are you joking? This is my life and my children are stuck in the middle. I must get them home and I cannot fathom any other reality." I continued to vent, "This is not fair. This sucks and I need more support from you on this."

"Scott, life is simply not always fair. Look outside your world for a moment and see what happens to people every day. Murders, rape, robbery, and stealing are not fair, but they happen every day."

His statement paralyzed me as I sat motionless. I continued to look around his office, temporarily stunned and thinking, as I had no reply.

I stared at him and then looked away, repeating this over and over. No words were spoken for what seemed to be five minutes, but probably lasted only a few seconds, when I finally broke the silence. "I appreciate your candor, but I don't like it."

"What Liza has done is terrible and your children are now far away. I just want you to look at all of the possible outcomes and realize that you may not get them back."

I told him that I felt completely confused but determined as I paced about his office, but that I would sure as hell figure out some way to bring them home.

I struggled to move forward, and John's words remained in the forefront of my mind. "You can't do this" was the most common response given to me by those who heard my story, and he agreed.

I would challenge some by asking, "Why?" Most would tell me that it was impossible or that I'd get myself killed, though they offered little in the way of specifics. They, too, were frightened and did not like being placed in this tough scenario with little chance of winning. I'd reply, "So then, come up with a scenario that has me back in Milwaukee with my children."

Unfortunately for me, I had stumped most of those I spoke with and had received little in the way of real tangible options except for Cliff.

Ten weeks had now passed. I felt stronger than I did the first few weeks.

Some suggested that I use reason to convince Liza to bring them home. I tried, but she didn't listen.

On a rare occasion in which she spoke with me on the phone I asked, "Liza, could we trade years with the kids? You'll have them one year and I'll have them the next?" I wasn't serious about this but I figured I might get my hands on them this way.

"No, Scott," she'd say. "The children are fine and they miss you. You can come and visit anytime you want. I'll let ya see them, don't worry. We're just not coming home, that's all. I hate my life there, so that is that."

I tried to work on her emotions. "When was the last time you liked your life? Don't you miss me? Don't you love me?"

"Yes I love you, but I can't go back there, Scott. I would rather be here with my family and the children than in America with the four of us."

I never did get an answer as to when she was last happy.

Any time I had a few minutes to talk with her, she would interrupt me in mid-thought or talk over me. It was nearly impossible to have a conversation that way. When I asked her what she would do if I had done such a thing to her, she replied, "I guess we'll never know now, will we?"

Ice cold, confident, and nestled in her cozy home so very far away from me with her parents, this thirty-two-year-old soon to be ex-wife of mine was letting me have it but good. I got nowhere, and she again refused to let me speak with our children.

I had reluctantly concluded that no clear channels were open for me to secure my children's safe return. Time moved both painfully slow and yet all too quickly. Scouring articles in magazines and newspapers in the library until closing offered a bit of insight, though I didn't find much. I could find even less with regard to men in my situation.

As I shuffled along each day my desperate feelings began to get replaced by extreme resolve and focus. Pissed off and determined, I was also very frightened. The thought of losing my kids for good left me more vulnerable than I had ever imagined. I sat alone at home eating dinner and wondering, "What if the majority of opinions are correct?"

If I failed to come up with a plan and execute it flawlessly, my little ones would never come home. I might live the remainder of my days a broken and lonely man.

I flashed back to bath time and smiled as I remembered how many toys they played with in the water. We applied extra baby shampoo to their heads and made funny shapes with their hair. The wall would be covered with suds and we would assist them in cleaning it off by holding the shower massage. Their great personalities and laughter infused with cute, chubby faces was a constant reminder of what I had to lose.

◆ ◆ ◆

CHAPTER 4

THE LIGHT BULB GLOWS BRIGHTLY

◆◆◆

ONE NIGHT AROUND midnight, I went to bed and cried inconsolably. I was tired, weak and so sad. The next morning I rolled out of bed, put my feet on the ground for thirty seconds or so and tried to find the strength to get up. Eventually I stood and headed toward the bathroom. I stared in the mirror for a minute or so. I had three days of beard and curls reaching in every direction. I gazed at the picture of my children that I had taped on the wall just to the right of my reflection. Brushing my teeth, I looked back at my tired face, and suddenly I had a moment of crystal clear thought. As these moments were now scarce, I could easily recognize it when it popped into my head. *Oh my God, that just might work! Wait a minute. You've got to be nuts. No, no way. Yes, yes that's it!*

Little sleep, plenty of tears, lots of coffee, and a somewhat lucid mind had helped me devise a plan within 45 minutes.

Thankfully, that human glue that holds us physically and mentally together during periods of crisis still kept me in one piece.

Jumping up and down I danced some weird dance that would surely get me kicked off any talent show. Returning to the mirror I gazed at myself and saw my reflection smiling back at me. I shouted, "Holy shit, I think I've got it!"

While looking in the mirror, Liza's voice had come to me. I felt as if I were channeling her as she instructing me on the best course to take.

I paced around the house like "Rain Man" muttering things out loud that might appear to an outsider as the ravings of some lunatic. *Thanks, Liza.*

Of course! If I wanted to get the children home I'd have to go through Liza, not around her. It came to me as words or music might come to an artist.

I saw the fragile shell of a plan developing, although it contained some huge gaps. I would work hard to fill in most of these holes and put my plan into action.

I went to work and tried to focus on the conversations I had with clients. Doubt remained my constant friend but desire fell right alongside me, too. I continued plotting with every waking moment. For the first time since the shock of the kidjacking, I had a clear, focused direction.

She held most of the cards, was living half a world away with our children, and laughing in the safety of her parent's home. I'd have to make this all about her feelings, desires, and warped sense of reality.

As this was now a war in my mind, I had no shame for the things I thought or the plans I was preparing to put into action. Over and over, I heard her saying in my head, "Scotty, the kids and I are staying in Israel. We are not coming back. You are free to begin a new life without us. They need to be with their mother."

I asked her what would become of me, and as she loved to talk, I engaged her when she allowed. "You can come here and live in Israel," was her reply.

How would I make a living in their depressed economy? As I asked the question the lady who thought pretty highly of herself answered as if I were in the room: "If you come here you could work in a store or start your own business. You could see the kids, too. I'll let you see them on a weekend or when I'm busy."

I tried ending the conversations before too much of my disdain and anger showed. And so I heard it many more times, her unwavering need to be *back home*. "You're married and we have two precious kids. You are not single, for heaven's sake!"

When I inquired as to what the children would do without their father, she stated with authority, "They have their mother and that is more important. A father is not as necessary."

No one on Earth was going to stand between me and my children. Now red with anger and ready to hit anything that crossed my path, my core emotions boiled and I wasn't sure I had enough control to keep myself together.

So there it was. My choices, according to Liza, were to stay in the States without the children and her. *Or,* I could drop everything, quit my job, hop on a plane, and move to Israel to be with them, *when* she allowed. I could become part of her make-believe life, which would get me closer to our children. Trust had gone away forever and so was any chance of my acquiescing. I began wondering if her warped perspective also had us living happily ever after.

By this time Liza's father, who had seven kids of his own, became involved. I could hear him shouting directions to his daughter in the background.

The one time he agreed to speak with me, things heated up.

"Joseph, my children are without their father. Do you support what Liza has done, or will you be sending them home?"

"They are home, Scotty. They're here in Israel with their mother. You should come and see them. We miss you."

"Yes, I understand where they are. My question is whether or not you support Liza keeping them from me?"

His tone grew terse. "Scotty, I want them here too. Liza is more happy here than in America. I want you to come and live here in Israel. Stop this nonsense."

"I understand, Joseph. You once told me that it would be better for Liza and me to live in America. You said that we would have a better life and greater opportunity. What changed?"

Now taking control of my family as well as his, he replied, "I will not allow them to come to you. You may visit them here!"

I hadn't spoken to my children for over two months so I attempted to try through him instead of Liza. "May I please speak to the kids?"

He handed the phone to Yoni. He made it perfectly clear in his little voice that there they were not returning to the U.S. It was obvious to me that he had been manipulated. I felt crushed.

Liza laid out my options according to her world and her family/advisors. I had no job waiting for me in the town of Tiberius, and the Israeli economy was barely breathing.

Move to Israel. Move on? I had few choices, and this did not sit well with me. I realized that I had unresolved issues with anyone telling me what to do, but it became magnified in this case.

Move to Israel or move on. That did not mean that only two options existed, right? After all, Mr. Spock from *Star Trek* taught us that there was always another option. I had worked day and night to come up with a flawless plan that would allow me to reunite with my kids back home in Milwaukee. The plan would soon be tested.

Closing my eyes, I tried to picture myself waking my two sleepyheads and getting them ready for school every morning. I'd go to work, come home to greet them as they arrived from school and then make dinner. Homework (no math please) and some fun time would be followed by baths, a story, and off to bed.

I knew they'd be better balanced and stable, emotionally and psychologically, with me as their primary caregiver. Their mother filled their little heads with the desperate words of a person who actually believed they could handle adult topics. She told them everything, absolutely everything, with zero regard to age-appropriateness, and their little brains were getting quite confused. This continued wreaking havoc on their tiny souls as well, and I would not allow anyone to mess with our children. Not even their mother. Her constant manipulation for self-gratification was unbearable for me. The knowledge that I sat, powerless, some 6,200 miles away unable to stop her abuse, continued to gnaw at me.

Part of my decision had already been made, and the rest came to me as I gazed into my bathroom mirror. I decided to fight for them with all I had! I was going all in and I realized it could get bloody, but pushed to my limits, I now began to ready myself for a fight.

I was ready to attack! A passive individual by nature, I was a father first with a job to do. So I made the ultimate decision for my children's future as well as mine, with no further hesitation.

I became clearly focused on raising them alone back in the States. I'd be their father and mother right here at home. I'd play both roles as best as I could and leave my life on the sidelines until they were grown. Now, how to make this desire a reality continued to richly churn in my mind with every passing hour.

I held a few photos of my kids I had taken three months earlier and squeezed them tightly. I kissed them, smiled, and whispered, "Don't worry my loves, Daddy's coming to get you."

◆ ◆ ◆

CHAPTER 5

THE PLOT THICKENS AND THE STEEL WALL WEAKENS

◆ ◆ ◆

I HAD TO pick up my game and start an offensive that would fly under Liza's radar, which is exactly what I had began to do. I had the advantage of Liza not hating me for any past behavior; in fact, I was good to her. I remained laser-focused and schemed every waking hour, while she milled about trying to figure out who she had become and what she was going to do next.

Sure, there were emotions flying about and unbelievable behavior on her part, but I sensed no loathing of me. This allowed me a minute opening in which to operate. I tried calling more and she would simply not talk to me. The children were also scarce, and I could only guess as to what they were up to and where they might be after three months.

Finally, I had another brief phone conversation with Liza. To my surprise, she spoke in a mild tone and even began joking. I took this to mean that I could move forward ever so slightly, like a lion stalking its prey.

Within one week, we were talking every third day. Resting the phone between my left ear and shoulder I gratefully agreed to most everything she had to say, and she had a lot on her mind. Mostly related to her life, "Scotty, I'm bored. I'm having a challenging time with the children, and I can't find a job." Her nights were spent playing cards and backgammon with her family or heading into town to dance.

We talked every second time I called, and then a week later every time. I realized that this was great progress. Though it remained painfully slow for me, I kept maneuvering and advancing ever so slightly, doing everything I could to not remain stationary. Almost four months had passed since I held my children, but I had to pretend to be focused on Liza when speaking with her. Did she receive the flowers I'd sent? Yes, she did. And what about the letters I sent telling her how much I missed her and our children? She had read some of them and asked if I meant everything I said. My response, always, "Of course I do, my love."

Holding the phone with two fingers, I listened closely for any clue as to how I should proceed while she once again shared her views on world politics, Israel our children, America, her family, work, and how bored she would get. I studied her, bit my tongue and gently asked non-threatening questions as I continued to talk, "Are you taking the kids to the park to play? Have they made some nice new friends?"

I saw glimpses of her appearing without her ever-present three-inch-thick steel wall. Liza missed me, but not enough to hop on the next flight with our children back to the States. No way.

I continued telling her exactly what she wanted to hear. How much I missed her and loved her always came out of my mouth before asking how the children were, and she needed this. I sensed that she wasn't interested in discussing them at any length, but when the topic became about her, she appeared happy to use me as her therapist. She continued sharing her inner feelings with me, and while it was painful to listen to on several levels, it helped to build her ego. Unhappiness with her father and some of her siblings became a standard topic. Few friends to spend time with were another, and an occasional funny story about the children would sneak in as well. Apparently, Yoni had located most of his sister's "hot buttons" and was pushing them at will.

Each phone call brought me closer to my children. I could almost touch them. I continued to sympathize with whatever she had to say in an attempt to lower her guard even more. I continued to push my personal agenda of bringing our children home by allowing Liza to use me as her sounding board.

Oftentimes our talks were off topic. She'd mentioned travel, her family, the space program, movies, food, and other nonsense as she expounded on her own philosophical and political beliefs. I waited for her to make that closing point and bring it home, but she rambled on, seldom finishing a thought on any topic. It continued to be all about her, not so much about me or us. I chewed on these small sessions of communicating all the while taking notes, I now believed that I could succeed as long as I put the kids' interests first at all times while stroking their mother's ego ever so gently.

This proved to be a difficult undertaking, because the loving, trusting, and loyal Scott was predictably gone. I pretended at certain key moments to be slightly sympathetic toward her position, and she took the bait. Her defenses (and trust me,

Israelis are born with them at a heightened level) were continuing to lower ever so slightly.

Liza knew she had messed up and had not totally thought through the ramifications of her actions. She wanted things her way and her way alone without the added bother of reason or logic, and I was hoping to give her an abundance of alone time in the future to sort it all out.

Trust flew out the window, so I knew something positively that Liza did not: we were finished!

We were getting divorced and I was determined to fight intensely to the end to be in Milwaukee, Wisconsin raising the little ones. This was ironic, because Liza firmly believed her parenting skills were superior to most.

If I made a point on any given subject that appeared to be spot on, she'd simply say, "Aw, you don't know what you're talking about," as she had nothing else to offer to contradict my statement.

After our phone conversations ended, I'd close my eyes and begin picturing myself as a single parent raising two little kids on my own. Yoni's brown curls and Ally's red ones always made me smile when they bounced around on their heads. I focused on good times and figured that there would be no dating and plenty of school activities to keep us busy. Not to be denied, I envisioned a court giving custody to a father in the '90s. As this practice was in its infancy back then, I still believed a strong and compelling case would convince a judge to place the children with me. Mothers, for better or worse, were receiving the majority of time and placement with children in most U.S. courts.

An extra bit of strength I call my "fifth gear" appeared to be running smoothly, I was about to embark on a journey that seemed like a movie. Wife kidnaps children. Wife hides them in Israel in different locations and offers little or no contact with them. Wife has no intention of bringing them back home, and the little ones are clueless as to what is going on. Wife is not bound by law to bring them back. Husband is screwed.

A simple commitment between a man and a woman is all we had. A signed agreement to love, honor, and you know the rest. Wife threatens to sever ties with husband unless he moves to Tiberius, Israel, and even then no promises. Several of her family members told me not to bother coming, because Liza's mind was made up. Two of Liza's brothers are policemen, which did not sit well with me. For the moment, she remained safe at her parent's home with her big family and our kids surrounding her.

So many thoughts came to me when I walked from room to room at night. A man would seem the more likely candidate to snatch a child. But I was wrong. How in the world could she do this? I didn't hit her. I spoke kindly to her. I never cheated. Home at night, I held down a good job that was beginning to pay well.

Who was right depended on who you asked, but the gloves were off and I planned on standing alongside the children in the end. My primal anger never far away during these times, I fought hard to keep it in check by running and doing deep breathing exercises.

Sitting on my couch and staring off into space I wondered what drives a person to such extremes. I figured she had some serious psychological issues, but I did not fully understand how damaged the kids' mother was at that point. Too close to the ordeal or simply not trained in psychotherapy, I'd be witness to a much clearer professional view into Liza's troubled mind in the future.

Her behavior reminded me of my mother, which may be why we got together in the first place. I suppose she felt familiar to me on some level, and I equated this to love. I second-guessed myself for a time because Liza was very convincing and she was my wife, as well as our children's mother. I now understood that in her mind, the mother was everything to the children and the father simply a bit player to be used as she saw fit.

It became part of a painful daily process—a process of guessing, second, third, and fourth guesses, with little gained, or so it seemed. Desperate to be with my kids, I began making the kind of promises that we make under huge amounts of stress. "If I get them back, I'll be the best father ever. I will always be there for them."

◆ ◆ ◆

CHAPTER 6

MY PLAN TAKES SHAPE

◆◆◆

DETERMINED TO FIND a way to bring the kids home, I slept five hours a night for weeks on end plotting late into the evenings. Walking by our hallway mirror I noticed I looked like crap. I felt worse than how I looked, but a constant wave of hope and deep desire remained in the forefront of my mind. As a fearful father, I dreamed of being reunited with my children.

Thirteen weeks had passed since the horrible news. Cliff, my friend, and the attorney whose smoke-filled office I sat in for many hours, called to check on me from time to time. He approved of the direction I chose. I had prepared my plan of attack and my fifth gear was again running strong. I talked to so many kind people. I could read in their faces and see in their eyes a combination of a strong desire to want to aid me in my quest to reunite with my children and the sad, empty feeling of helplessness.

First, I had to lull Liza and anyone else who might report back to her into thinking that I sincerely wanted to move to

Israel. I filled out bogus immigration papers to give the impression that our family would soon be immigrating there. My hope was to show her how much I needed to be with her. If she ever questioned my motives or desire, I could easily prove it with the help of an unsuspecting Israeli official.

I decided to begin with a phone call to the *Shaliah* in Milwaukee. A Shaliah is a man or woman, often from Israel, who resides for a time in many different cities in America to help people legally immigrate to Israel.

Ari, the man I spoke with, appeared happy to help with all of my questions. He explained to me in broken English that he came from Be'er Sheva, and he would be happy to help a new prospect understand the laws and privileges as they pertained to immigrating to Israel.

As we sat in his small office I noticed the map of Israel, a country one eighth the size of Florida. Ari explained the guidelines and laws for immigrating and how much money, clothing, and furniture we could bring. As we sipped strong coffee he asked, "Why do you want to move to Israel now? It is hard to live there. I think things are much better here."

I couldn't be sure if he was really interested or just prodding as I composed myself and replied, "My wife wants to live there because she is Israeli, and I want to be with my wife. I have been there twice and love it."

I watched him taking notes. He seemed excited at the prospect of our moving to Israel. I listened to every word. I learned what papers needed to be completed and what types of identification would be required. I answered all of his questions and he gave me much needed information.

I called him twice a day for three days with questions so that he and anyone from Tiberius checking up on me would know I was serious. Yeah, I was plenty paranoid. I planned on telling Liza that I had been in touch with this man to begin making arrangements to move, hoping it would add a bit more credibility to my overall plan.

I needed good legal representation if my plan were to indeed work. I knew just who to call after talking to my mentor Cliff.

My cousin Marv was an attorney and a contemporary of Cliff's. I wasted no time calling him. His first words were, "You've got to be kidding me, Scott. When did this happen?"

I filled him in and added that I felt paralyzed by fear. "I didn't want to bother you because we are family. Sorry."

"Okay, I know what we can do. Come down to my office today and we'll talk."

Although Marv wanted to help, he couldn't take the lead chair in my case because of our family ties. Like Cliff, he too had significant connections and huge victories to his name, so who did I get to represent me? Julie, of course! A junior partner at Marv's firm, not Jewish, with no Israeli connections, but she had a tough and fearless quality much like Marv had in his younger years.

When Julie and I met for the first time, I noticed her warm smile and pretty face. She had some freckles around her nose and brown shoulder-length hair. Dressed in a grey business suit, she sat across from me at a large conference table. I explained in depth what had happened. She listened intently while taking notes, only looking up at me once in a while. I noticed a rubber band on her left wrist and asked her about it.

"It's something I've done since law school. It helps keep me relaxed in some way, I guess."

Julie appeared sharp and asked a lot of questions during our first meeting. Specializing in family law, she continued to take notes and when she paused I looked her straight in the eye. "Julie, I need an attorney who can be very tough. I need a pit bull to represent me. Are you that person?"

She smiled, "Yes, I can be aggressive and play hardball when it is necessary."

Now up and pacing around the room I continued, "You must assure me that you are the right attorney for the children and me. I must be convinced, because too much is riding on this. The fact that Marv thinks you can do this carries a lot of weight."

We continued to talk and go over strategies and I began to gain confidence in her abilities. Her calm exterior would be a good fit for my difficult situation. I saw in front of me an intelligent lady who was willing to get down in the mud when the time came.

"How are you going to get the kids on a plane without them kicking, screaming, and causing a huge scene?" she asked. "You could easily get arrested and thrown in jail. I can be of great help to you once you get them on American soil, but there is little I can do for you before that. There are papers we can file, but the children must be here for us to move the case forward."

Now sitting next to her I said, "Julie, Liza is both strong and weak. It is the weak part of her that I hope will make her vulnerable enough for me to influence. I've been planting seeds over the last couple of months, explaining that I could not live without her and the children. I'm still not with them and I'm deeply concerned for their well being. I even forced tears and lied through my teeth trying to convince her that I would live anywhere as long as we could be together as a family."

"I looked in romance books and read magazines looking for the right combination of words to soften her hard exterior, and I think it's working. I've made some progress talking to her the last few weeks, too. She's had ample time to think and has had the children for quite some time now. I sense she's bitten off a lot and is lonely, confused, and never quite happy with her family. When we talk, Liza opens up and uses me as her therapist and confidant. I bite my tongue, listen to everything she says, and I say very little. I don't want to piss her off, so I agree with almost everything. My phone bills are in the hundreds of dollars."

Julie listened intently and continued taking notes. I went on, "I'm hoping that these kind and gentle words get through to her on an emotional level, though I'm being careful not to sell it too much. She wants the storybook ending, but I had already offered that by sweeping her off her feet, marrying her, and bringing her to the U.S., as she wanted. If I could convince Liza of this completely, she might volunteer to get back on a plane to the States with our kids. If she or any of her family sense that I am not being one hundred percent genuine, the show is over. I have primed her and can tell she is halfway there. The rest will have to be done in person."

"Scott, you're telling me that you plan on going to the Middle East into a possibly hostile environment alone? You'll have no guarantee of success. You do realize that this could get ugly really fast, don't you? I mean, you could get hurt, or worse. I can't protect you or the children from here if this goes south."

"Yep, I know," I said, forcing a smile. "Want to join me?"

Her kind yet cautious grin reminded me of some of the people I had talked to in the past. I could sense she felt the same as others regarding my slim chances, though she tried not to let on.

"Julie, I have been and am still very open to suggestions. Have you discussed this with Marv?"

She appeared somber. "Yes, I have. We have called associates and racked our brains to think of another option and we are, unfortunately, at a loss. Legally, she is not bound to return to America with your children. I'm sorry, Scott."

"Don't be sorry—just be ready in case I pull this off. I'll hopefully need your representation and Marv's input big time in the near future." I explained that once my family came back to the U.S., I would need two days to recuperate from jet lag before serving Liza with divorce papers. Raising my eyebrows I said, "That's when the shit is going to hit the fan."

She assured me that she would have the papers ready.

"I intend to get Liza's permission to visit her and our children. This will take more maneuvering, but she is speaking with me almost every day. In the end, I'll have to ask the Queen for an audience. How humiliating!"

"My plan is to fly over there and back with the three of them within one week. Although I'll need to recuperate from jet lag, I don't want to stay long in Tiberius because I view it as a lion's den. Also, I'm scared to death."

When we were finished Julie shook my hand, smiled, wished me good luck and told me to call her the minute I arrived back in Milwaukee with my children. "You know what, scratch that, Scott. Please call me when you land in Chicago. Don't worry about the time."

I left her office felling more confident than I had in weeks. Julie had convinced me that she could handle my case and give me a good shot at winning custody of my children.

As I got into my car, I stared up into the still grey sky. I contemplated just how far I had progressed over the last four months. I also reminded myself that nothing could be guaranteed, especially in the Middle East. I still had the most difficult part of my journey ahead of me.

◆◆◆

CHAPTER 7

ALL IN

◆◆◆

I COULD HARDLY comprehend what might await me in Israel. Having little to no leverage didn't help matters, as my mind once again began playing out the many possible scenarios. Would I be welcomed with open arms by Liza and our children? Would Liza call the police or get her cop brothers involved? Would I get killed and buried in the Negev Desert? Did Israel have Child Protective Services and, if so, whose side would they be on? I wouldn't have to wait much longer to find the answers.

I continued to check in with family and friends, seeking advice. Saying "no" to ideas they presented was making progress too, as it allowed me to streamline my thought process.

The mercenary idea, though a bust, did provide me and others with a few laughs during tense times. I had a lot of ideas and none were too bizarre to me, including having Liza "disappear." I kept jotting down more and more of them on paper, while putting an "X" though those I presumed would land me in a foreign jail or worse.

At night, I laid my head on my pillow and listened to the sounds of our empty house. It was eerily quiet except for the usual rustling of the trees outside. Staring up at the ceiling, I thought about playing catch or hide-and-seek with Jonathan. Who was playing my role? I wondered. I wanted so badly to enter their rooms and give them a kiss and hug, read a story, and goof around with them.

Weeks were now months. I had planned hard and prepared well to get my kids back. Gone were the painful days of scheming. Liza had softened up enough over five months to allow me to visit her. Realizing that this was the most serious and possibly dangerous situation I had ever encountered, my focus became stronger. Regrettably, I had no training in retrieving and returning little kids from far-off lands.

Although I didn't feel up to scaling this Everest alone, I quickly realized that I had no choice. I had the most to lose, and remained determined to hold on tightly to both of them if I ever got them back.

I was all in.

I never located a manual for this journey. No "how-to" book to read. I looked everywhere. I just had to develop a foolproof plan. I knew that I was in uncharted waters. It was rough and I tend to get seasick.

It didn't take long for me to realize that, wounded or otherwise, it would be up to me to bring my children home. If I wanted them back, I had to go and get them myself. Dreams of a speedy ending had faded and the kids were no closer to me.

So I went to get them.

◆ ◆ ◆

CHAPTER 8
ISRAEL BOUND

◆ ◆ ◆

TWO WEEKS HAD passed since my first meeting with Julie and eighteen weeks since Liza left with our children. It took over four months before she granted me permission to visit her and our children in Tiberius. Although unsure of what she wanted from our marriage, I knew Liza had zero doubt in her mind where she was going to live.

It had been too long since I last held my children. I spent evenings mostly alone so that I could rehearse my role over and over in my head. Fearful of stumbling, I made up questions they might ask and had answers to every one of them. Friends and family quizzed me in person and over the phone. I stayed up late rehearsing with a hot pot of coffee at the ready.

All about Liza, I kept reminding myself as I continued to rehearse every possible scenario that could be thrown my way. Sitting in our cozy back yard watching the birds dart in and around our bird feeder, I asked myself difficult questions. I had to make her feel as if she was the main topic and not our children, or she would quickly back away. How would her family react when they saw me? I knew that she had filled their heads with lies. Would they try to stop me from seeing the kids or coming to their home? What would Liza's father say to me? How did my little ones look? They must have grown. How would they react when they saw me? Did Ally have longer red curls? Did Jonathan still have his great laugh? Will I be greeted with warm hugs from them or will a chill have settled in?

Then, after what seemed like forever, I drove to Chicago and hopped on a jet to Tel Aviv.

◆ ◆ ◆

CHAPTER 9
A BUMPY ROAD

◆◆◆

PERHAPS FATE WAS smiling on me as I made my way to my exit row aisle seat I had requested. A packed DC-10 settled in for a 13 hour flight.

We had been in the air for an hour when a flight attendant walked by. "Hello," he said, "Would you care for a beverage?"

Reflecting on my life and what brought me to make this long trip, my eyes were focused somewhere outside on the wing of the plane. He tapped me gently on the shoulder and I looked up with a blank expression.

"You seem to be deep in thought. Would you care for something to drink?"

"Yes, please. A glass of water and a glass of apple juice would be great. Thanks."

He brought the drinks. I took a few sips and continued to think about how I got myself into this enormous mess in the first place.

◆◆◆

In 1984, at the age of 25, I decided to take a trip to Europe. I had come into a bit of money from an inheritance and always loved the idea of seeing the world. I can't remember a time when I didn't want to travel, so travel I did.

Near the end of my two-month journey, I met a woman named Liza (pronounced Leeza). A year later we were married. We had two wonderful kids: Jonathan and Alexandra. We called them Yoni (Johnny in Hebrew) and Ally. So excited to find a partner who would give me the opportunity to experience all that marriage had to offer, I leaped into our relationship. She was so charming, a petite 5'3" with long brown curls and a full-of-life personality. She had a contagious energy and never stopped to sit for long. I knew that I had made the right decision, and Liza felt the same.

I could not imagine in a million years that she'd take our children, destroying my life in the process.

Like many, I had my share of difficulties growing up. My parents were troubled. My father committed suicide when I was 15 years old and my mother had anger issues, to put it mildly. And I discovered that I had Attention Deficit Disorder.

I was born in Milwaukee, Wisconsin on January 25, 1959, the youngest of three children, to Stan and Eileen Lesnick. My sister, Carole, six years older, and a brother, Bruce, four years older. We have been through many things together, as siblings often are.

We grew up in the '60s and '70s in a middle-class family with some nasty secrets. I didn't know that my father was a compulsive gambler. He blew most of the money we had. A kind man who loved Vegas and the stock market so much that he became a stockbroker. Probably not a good idea, but it did keep him close to other people's money, which I presume is what he wanted. A mild-mannered man, he married an overbearing lady.

Mom was a second generation American. She came from some money that my grandparents made in the retail clothing and credit business. She loved the finer things in life, a trait I also inherited. Dad was out of her league and knew it. He needed a kinder, gentler wife to go along with his mellow personality.

With money at the forefront of their relationship, things turned bad. There were plenty of fights. We were middle class and living well, so I didn't realize that things were getting ugly between my parents. I later learned that my father amassed huge debt and was partially bailed out by my maternal grandfather, Max. It was Max who kept us in our home, never asking for a thing in return.

Our father tried to provide well for our mother. However, he approached it in the wrong way, which almost caused the demise of our family and our home.

One spring day I came home from school to find police cars and an ambulance in our driveway. My dad had killed himself. I was sixteen years old. No note and no closure. That hurt so much. We'd been close, and I still needed his guidance in my life.

I was ripe for learning and reluctant to ask much from my mom. Also, my dad had helped protect us from our mother's wicked temper. Bruce and Carole were away at college. I lived at home, left to contend with my mother's violent moods.

I continued to grow and soon became too large for Eileen to physically assault. My fears of getting hit with hard objects finally dissipated when I realized that I could take her down hard if necessary. This was a huge relief for a boy who had lived in fear of having a pan tossed in his direction, or worse. Mom liked to hit and yell. She used pots and pans, belts and shoes with heels, too. She made me stand in a corner taking whatever physical punishment she felt like giving that day. Her brutal behavior toughened me up. In the future, I'd have to stay strong under enormous pressure.

My sister bore the brunt of our mother's wrath. Bruce and I received our share, too. Growing up, we had no idea how to defend ourselves against an abusive parent. Although certainly not professionals, we figure that our mother had a bipolar disorder along with sociopathic tendencies.

We learned how to read people. We'd listen to the sound of her footsteps to see how much weight she was placing on them. The more noise, the farther away you wanted to be. Too young and often too late in reading her mood, I paid the price.

I learned a valuable lesson—to be kind and gentle to my own children. I constantly told myself that I would raise my kids in an atmosphere of love and trust, not fear. Instead of being an abusive parent, I made the clear decision early on to be a safe and caring parent. Sure, I could shoot that fatherly glare in their direction or yell a bit. However, corporal punishment and brutality were not options. Only hugs and lots of talking would be allowed. Even at their young ages Yoni and Ally knew that any topic, no matter what, was open for discussion with me.

Mom made it to age 50 and died of breast cancer.

She did instill two things in me. The first was to always finish what I started. The second was that I could do anything I wanted *if* I fully applied myself. Lastly, she did love her children. She just possessed a painful way of showing it.

Growing up, I realized that older people knew much more than I did. I listened, learned and took some great lessons from them. My grandmother Eve taught me gentleness and honesty. I also learned to listen and respect, while trying not to judge too much.

◆◆◆

I held the El Al airlines magazine in my hands. I had it open to a page showing the turquoise waters of the Caribbean. Smiling at the beach life, I finished my drinks, ate some snacks and tried to get some sleep. I couldn't rest because I was too nervous about my long flight and what awaited me in Tel Aviv. I glanced at the pictures of my children, kissed them and placed them by my heart. I looked for strength, took some deep breaths and continued to assess my life.

◆◆◆

My grandfather Max taught me to love music and how to sell most anything. He showed me that it was OK to laugh at yourself and others. He saw the salesman in me early and nurtured it.

We all grew up and moved out of our house as quickly as we could.

I went to Miami, Florida for college, a carnival-like atmosphere in the late '70s and early '80s. Unfortunately, I had no one guiding me. I could have used a father at that time. I had fun and attended only select classes, which wasted my mother's money.

In 1981 after college, I moved to New York City to work as an assistant to a gentleman named Chuck, a clothing representative for Calvin Klein Women's Apparel. These were magical times. I shared a modest two-bedroom apartment with a lady in her late twenties named Susan in Kew Gardens, Queens. I sold a hot line of clothing: women's jeans. The line and the name opened doors. I serviced smaller family-type stores and became lost many times while trying to navigate my way around the boroughs of New York.

I lasted eighteen months before telling Chuck I couldn't afford to work for him anymore. Between my lackluster sales and modest income, I couldn't pay my rent.

My mom was now dying from breast cancer, so I headed home to help her. I lived at home and helped hospice make her comfortable. She died a month later.

Bruce and Carole lived out of town but stayed in close touch. They did come to help, but the majority of the daily care fell on hospice and me. This is when the age difference between we three siblings began to blur; no longer the little brother, we were becoming equals.

Because of growing up in a harsh environment, we promised to be there for one another. Carole had protected me against our mother's rage at times, by deflecting it onto herself and bearing the brunt of it. I like to think that if the tables were turned I'd have done the same.

Emotions were plentiful, and I missed not having my father there to help me through this difficult and guilt-ridden time.

I moved back to Milwaukee to regroup. I felt like I had let

myself down with my mom's passing. In any case, something positive did occur. Each kid was left a tidy sum of money from her estate. I didn't blow it all right away, choosing instead to tuck some away for a rainy day. Also, remembering my father's lack of success with money and all of the pain it caused us helped me keep things in proper prospective. Later, I would use some of the money for a down payment on my first house.

I continued to search for the true me, unaware of any particular strength I possessed. I'd get by, giving a decent effort while hoping for maximum gain, unwilling to put myself out there all the way. I knew people who did give their all, and I admired their ability to do so.

◆ ◆ ◆

Now in my early thirties on my third trip to Tel Aviv, I smiled at another flight attendant as she handed me dinner. Three hours had passed since we'd taken off from Chicago's O'Hare International Airport. I began to pick at my meal, dissecting the chicken, trying to figure out what type of stuffing was inside. I couldn't read the books I brought along. My mind kept wandering; I realized that I had been pushed to my very limits as a human being.

◆ ◆ ◆

CHAPTER 10

IS THAT AN UZI, MA'AM?

◆◆◆

NOW OVER THE Atlantic Ocean, I continued examining the decisions that led me on my dire journey.

As far back as I can remember I have loved traveling. The world outside the States intrigued me. My friends were either busy or short of money, so I decided to take a trip to Europe by myself. Europe at twenty-five offered more than I could dream of, and I gave myself two months to see the world and have some fun. Add to this a bit of money from my mother's estate and good times were bound to happen.

I knew I'd meet interesting people and discover more about myself. If I was lucky, even find out where I fit in the world. I wanted to have fun! I imagined so many possibilities. Who would I meet? How would the food taste? What might I see? Can you really party freely in Amsterdam? Just how beautiful is Paris?

Living on a shoestring budget, I traveled parts of England, France, the Netherlands, Greece and Italy. In London I met a local named Farida, who happily showed me around her wonderful city. She was a nice young lady with long brown hair, plenty of charm, and a neat accent. We dined in quaint English pubs and walked around her city for three days, hitting all the high points.

After England, I made my way to Amsterdam and Paris. Two weeks later I landed in the south of France. I met up with Andrew, Richard and Lynn, all fellow travelers in search of some adventure. We decided to travel together and did so for four weeks. We had a wonderful time as we made our way through France, Italy and Greece.

Our time to say good-bye to each other came. The four of us walked into a travel agent's office in Athens with our luggage in tow and instantly saw the huge world map on the wall. We just stared at it with big grins on our faces. The thought of viewing the planet spread out on a wall and choosing any place I wanted to go was intoxicating.

Athens provided all of us with one crucial element: an international airport that could take you in any direction you chose. I planned to head back through Switzerland, Austria, and who knew where else. As I looked at the map again, something hit me. *I'm Jewish.* "How long does it take to fly from Athens to Tel Aviv?" I asked the travel agent.

"About an hour and a half," he answered.

"That's all? I could be in the Mideast in an hour and a half?"

All I had to do was purchase the ticket and hop on a plane. Never mind that I only spoke five words of Hebrew and knew know one in the country. I came to Europe not knowing anyone. My confidence now soaring, I knew I'd meet people.

The bittersweet moment came to say farewell to my friends.

I chose to do the group farewell so as not to tear up. A month after meeting each other in Nice, we headed off to new lands not knowing that my choice, Israel, would change my life forever.

The plane ride from Athens to Tel Aviv was quick and exciting. People were dressed in Middle Eastern and European styles, which added a wonderful flavor to the flight. Some wore religious clothing with colorful scarves on their heads. I wore a pair of shorts and a tee shirt from the Hard Rock Café, with a pair of Stan Smith tennis shoes. Smoking was still permitted on most flights. A thick smoky haze hung over the main cabin, and a variety of languages could be heard.

I stood up to check out the crowd as I slowly walked toward the rear of the aircraft. In the aisle, Jews and Muslims were busy getting closer to their gods through prayer as I awkwardly attempted to make my way to the bathroom.

Once again, new customs were right before my eyes waiting for me to absorb. The world became smaller as I quietly observed these ancient customs and languages.

As we approached Tel Aviv, I felt an emotional burst of warmth and joy. I had absolutely no idea why this happened to me. When we landed I had tears in my eyes.

Israel has a deep and powerful hold on Jews and non-Jews alike, and I was pulled in too. A man in his 60s sitting across from me said that this occurs to some people as they near the Holy Land.

Not being very religious, I wondered if I missed the friends I had left in Europe or if maybe I was homesick. The death of my mom still churned in my mind. Could it be the land itself? No matter; upon landing, a huge outburst of clapping, loud singing, and other sounds of joy filled the plane. Blown away by this show of utter bliss by people so happy to be here, I smiled and clapped along.

It was October 1984 and the most important Jewish holiday of Yom Kippur would begin in a little less than a week. I needed to get acquainted with my surroundings before most of the country shut down for two days.

Adrenalin flowed through me as our plane pulled up to the terminal. We stopped short of the gate, the stairs came down, and we disembarked directly toward solders with machine guns. Warmth from the Mideast sun hit my face. I felt nervous at the sight of those guns. No one had warned me that young people my age would be carrying Uzis and pistols. Not looking for any trouble I figured I'd just act normal. "This show of might is for everyone's protection," said a nice lady when I inquired.

"I didn't know that we need protection. What's going on?"

"They want to make sure that there are no terrorist attacks. Is this your first time in Israel?" I nodded. "Don't be too alarmed," she said with a lovely accent. "This is common here and rarely do they need to use them."

I rationalized that many more people are killed in America every day than in Israel.

I stepped out of the airport doors into crowds of people looking for families. Once again, young men and women mingled among us with loaded weapons. The soldiers, of all ages, looked like our neighbors back home in any state. I found out later that they had many of the same interests as we do but they grew up in a land of intense, ongoing conflict.

Since Israel is such a small country I traveled all over in a short amount of time while seeing fantastic sights. Not far from the airport, I decided to make Jerusalem my first stop.

I shared a taxi to the city center and was blown away by the sights and sounds. My driver spoke English and pointed out some of the more famous landmarks along the way. With our windows down, the smells immediately aroused my senses. I smiled while being bombarded with so much to see. Vendors sold food and clothing, and there were makes and models of cars I did not recognize.

Tired and overwhelmed, I stayed close to the hotel that evening and had dinner at a falafel stand. My first time eating this messy yet delicious meal, I quickly became a fan. After a beer, I returned to my room to watch a little local TV and relax.

The next morning I walked around Jerusalem and the old walled city. I felt like I had transported back in time. The sounds, sights, and smells again overwhelmed my senses. I walked up to the Wailing Wall and saw thousands of little notes packed tightly in the cracks as people prayed or stood in silence. Strolling for another two hours, I toured ancient tunnels and became twisted around as I tried to make my way toward the Damascus gate.

My day ended with a visit to the Dome of the Rock on the Temple Mount. Afterward, I slowly made my way out of the Jewish Quarter trying to capture every sight and sound that I could before heading out of the old walled city.

Back at my hotel, I made plans to catch an early morning bus to Eilat at the bottom of the country on the Red Sea. At 5:30 a.m., after a less than stellar sleep, I awoke, showered, collected my belongings, and checked out.

The city of Jerusalem was slowly beginning to wake from a better night's rest than I had. I made my way to the central bus station. I heard sweet sounds coming from mosques and other houses of worship. I smelled bread and other assorted baked goods coming from bakeries as I walked to the bus stop. Hungry, I picked up some provisions for my trip and made it just as the bus pulled up. I purchased a round trip ticket and boarded, quickly picking an aisle seat near the front. Shoving ensued as people yelled and pushed to find a seat.

My journey took me to the Dead Sea, where we stopped at a beautiful oasis for a break and a swim. The sun burned extremely hot and the water felt slimy as I waded in at the lowest elevation on the planet. The few cuts I had on my hands quickly found the abundance of salt as I proceeded to lie on my back on and above the water. Small waves splashed about and some accumulations of salt formed mounds near the shore that looked like ice.

When I emerged, I had a thick coating of what I called sea slime all over me except for my face. There were showers for rinsing off, and mud baths as well.

We continued on toward Eilat, passing Bedouin families in the desert. The adventure of a lifetime continued to play out before my eyes, and I enjoyed the ride. Could I be any closer to so many neat countries? Egypt and Jordan, with Syria and Lebanon to the north.

We arrived at Eilat. I didn't know where to go so I asked a cab driver for suggestions. He recommended a nice hotel, because I wanted to relax and enjoy this wonderful seaside resort in modern comfort. Most of my beds thus far had been a bit lumpy, and I often shared a room and toilet with others. He said that the King Solomon hotel was popular with Israelis and tourists as well, so off we drove.

My large room at the hotel overlooked a beautiful pool and

had its own shower and cozy bed. I plopped my stuff on the floor and decided to nap for a few hours before dinner. When I awoke, the sun had already set and I momentarily forgot where I was, an eerie feeling, even if just for five seconds. I showered and headed out to tour my home for the next several days. I went to the small city center to find some food and soak in the local scene. Seafood was abundant so I pigged out and had a few Maccabi beers.

Some people suggested I try snorkeling in the Red Sea. So clear was the water you could see ten feet in front of you to the bottom, they explained. They spoke about beautiful coral reefs and an underwater observatory; that was all I needed to hear.

The next morning I awoke refreshed and relaxed as I looked out my window to another sunny day. After eating, I changed into my bathing suit and headed to the beach across the street. The view astounded me. Jordan lay across the water. At my feet, the beautifully clear Red Sea just begged me to dive in, so I did.

With rented mask and snorkel firmly in place, I found myself instantly surrounded by the most wonderful sea life as I moved slowly back and forth. At 10 a.m. the sun was hot, but that did not stop dozens of people from hitting the beach and finding a spot in the shade.

One hour felt just right for the first day as I slowly made my way out of the sea. I found a cozy shade tree to sit under, and I proceeded to drink a quart of water. People played *mat cot* on the hot sand, a game with two paddles and a rubber ball. I made my way back to the hotel to shower and change. I decided to head down to the gift shop to buy a pack of cigarettes and some gum.

Exiting the elevator, I scoped out the luxurious lobby, then made a couple of lefts and found the gift shop—and my future wife.

◆ ◆ ◆

CHAPTER 11

LIZA

◆ ◆ ◆

LIZA SAT BEHIND a large glass counter doing paperwork when she looked up. I immediately noticed her big brown eyes and long brown curly hair. She smiled. I returned a smile and asked for a pack of Marlboros in my limited Hebrew. She replied in good English, "You speak Hebrew well."

"Come on, I can't even form a sentence. You, however speak English very well. My name is Scott, what's yours?"

"Scotty, I like that name. My name is Liza."

We continued to chat in my native tongue. She was twenty-five, charming, and had a contagious laugh. She had been working at the hotel for about three months.

We talked for forty-five minutes with only two customers interrupting our conversation. I asked what prompted her to come to Eilat.

"I decided to get out of Tel Aviv for a while because it was too busy. I wanted to be with tourists and Eilat is so beautiful. I finished the army a few years ago and now I am enjoying life on my terms. How long do you plan on staying here?"

"I only arrived yesterday. It's not like I imagined. It's beautiful and remote at the same time. I have no definite plans, but I'll be heading back to Tel Aviv within a week."

I instantly liked her and thought she felt the same way, so I asked her if she wanted to get together after work.

"Well, I've been talking to you for almost an hour. Do you think I'm going to say no?" This petite woman with energy for three agreed to go out with a not-so-strange man.

I made my way back to the gift shop at eight and waited until she finished closing. She wore a big smile and began talking to me a mile a minute. We decided to go out for a bite and get to know each other. Seafood was the meal, soda was the drink, and fine was the conversation.

Liza appeared very direct, very open, and had a good sense of humor. I learned that she thought of herself as a self-proclaimed "independent woman" who liked astrology, dressed in tight clothes, and loved to dance.

Her accent, coupled with her English, made for a pleasant sound so I just sat back and listened. She spoke her mind on a variety of subjects.

"Liza, are all Israelis so direct and open with their thoughts and opinions?"

"Look," she explained, "we never know what is going to happen in life, and that goes double if you live here, so we tend to get right to the point."

We laughed and strolled by the water until 1 a.m., stopping for some drinks and dancing. She reminded me that she had to be at work at 9 a.m. I didn't want the night to end and I could tell she felt the same, so we agreed to see each other the next day. I walked her to her door and gave her a kiss on the cheek.

She laughed. "Come on, you can do better than that!" And so I did. I enjoyed our extended kiss as she reached up on her tiptoes to meet me halfway.

The next day I picked her up at four and we walked hand-in-hand for hours along the water, eventually stopping for dinner. I could feel the chemistry—we were both enjoying every moment. Liza looked at me and leaned in closer. "I can't believe how happy I am, being with you. Men have not always been who I hoped they'd be. Did I say that well?"

"Yes, you did." I gently put my hand on her cheek. "I understand and I am happy, too. Are you going to make me go dancing again?" I asked with a smile.

"Yes. You're in good shape. Can't you keep up with me, you poor boy?"

"I believe I can, ma'am. I just don't dance much, but I'll definitely make an exception in your case."

Five romantic days later, I told her that I would be heading back to Tel Aviv. She asked if I would like to see where she was from and I quickly said yes.

"I'll need to work one more day and then I will be able to get some days off. Is that okay with you?"

"Of course it is!" I exclaimed, and 36 hours later we took a bus to Tel Aviv and made our transfer to the bus heading to Tiberius on the Sea of Galilee. We arrived in Tel Aviv around 5 a.m. to a city that had just begun to wake up. We ducked into a café to have a bite along with some much-needed coffee. Liza shared with me her uneasiness with her life and said that she had difficulty staying in one place for an extended period of time. "I think I'm always searching for the right fit in my life, know what I mean, Scotty?"

"I'm not sure. Tell me more."

"I know I can be happy, and I want a family one day, but I never found the right person."

She gave me a huge smile and put her hand on mine. I sensed her openness and a real desire to connect with me on a deep emotional level. Our bus didn't leave until 7 p.m., so we decided to take a walk along the seldom quiet streets.

◆ ◆ ◆

My plane hit a pocket of turbulence. Momentarily stunned, I got up from my seat to use the bathroom and stretch my legs. Another hour had passed. I was now halfway to Israel. Washing my hands, I looked in the mirror and gave myself a half-hearted smile. I looked like crap. I slowly walked back to my seat, catching glimpses of everyone sleeping. I envied them.

◆ ◆ ◆

Liza slept on my shoulder as the bus made its way to Tiberius. The Sea of Galilee appeared a beautiful blue, and a short cab ride up the steep hills brought us to her home.

Her family was welcoming and, thankfully for me, spoke English well. We began to get to know one another as each took their turn asking a number of questions.

They had a modest home in the hills above the sea that, through careful planning, slept nine. Liza and I drank tea and ate some cake with her family. All six brothers and sisters were around. I felt intimidated as everyone crammed into the dining room.

Liza wanted to show me her town, so we borrowed her dad's car and drove to the city center. The steep and winding roads made breaking any land records impossible.

People went about their daily lives while walking within feet of beautiful ancient ruins. Hebrew, Arabic, English and French were spoken on the streets as we made our way to a seaside café for a drink.

I spent three days with her family and got to know them. Her mother came from Cairo, her father from Casablanca. Mom had black hair and a kind, gentle smile. The abundance of food made sure no one would go hungry. She ran the home and managed to raise seven children.

Liza's dad worked in construction as a foreman. He had an intimidating stare, a tough smile, a strong frame and a thin mustache. He was old-school and happy to have a visitor from afar. We hit it off right away, which made everyone more comfortable.

The second oldest of seven and the same age as me, Liza had a close relationship with her family. By this time we had been together for a week, and there was no doubt that we had the major hots for each other. She shared with me her love for the States and wanted to check out where I lived. The issue of my returning home to find a job became a priority. She didn't want me to go and I didn't want to leave, but we agreed that it would be good for us if I could find work and bring her over to visit. We said our long, tearful goodbye. I made my way back to Ben Gurion International Airport to head home.

◆ ◆ ◆

CHAPTER 12

MILWAUKEE 1984

◆◆◆

MY FANTASTIC TWO month trip overseas ended a few weeks earlier than planned as I flew back to Chicago and took the bus up to Milwaukee. Liza called the next day. It was great to hear her voice. "I miss you already. When are you coming back?"

"I need to get a job. Perhaps you'd come here to visit? It's beautiful and we have a big lake like the one you grew up on, only it's a lot colder here."

We talked for an hour. Long distance telephone plans to the Middle East were not too generous back in the mid-'80s. She happily agreed to make plans to come visit. "I thought you'd never ask."

I assured Liza that I'd make arrangements to bring her over soon. I had a one-bedroom apartment on Milwaukee's east side and loved the area. I took my time looking for work, until one afternoon my friend Bobby came over. I answered the door and watched as he stood there shocked, just staring at my red sweat pants and an undershirt. "Buddy, what in the hell are you doing?"

"I'm watching TV. Why?"

"You need to get off your ass and go get a job," he said in an uncharacteristically stern tone.

He was right, but I had zero prospects. I was in love and had some money, so there didn't seem to be any urgency.

Bobby got me an interview with Bob Gorecki, a manager at Shaw Industries, which literally changed my life forever. He allowed me to jump into the manufacturer's representative business selling carpet to stores around Wisconsin. After two interviews and a quick trip down south to Ringgold, Georgia, they offered me my own territory. I gladly accepted.

I took some of my previously learned skills and put them to work. I worked long hours, with guidance from Bob developing my sales skills. A friend of mine called it "learn as you go."

Older and often wiser with regards to selling, my competition ran circles around me. The difficult task of trying to sell when others like me were better played on my ego, but I didn't give up. I spent many nights plotting on how I might outsell the other reps. I thought about Liza. I looked for weaknesses in their skills and took notes on each. Like many of us, they enjoyed talking about themselves. I used this all-too-human trait to train myself in the finer points of selling, and I also picked their brains when they allowed. Some were more open than others, so I gravitated toward them.

Three months passed when things began to click for me. My peers noticed me more and so did my company. Bob always said, "Scotty, I want to clone you." This felt wonderful because much of sales has to do with recognition and, of course, closing the deal.

Most work days, I hit the road by 9 a.m. and usually made five to six calls a day. I was in charge of who and how many customers I saw each day. Somewhat surprised, I became a self-motivated individual who used his time wisely.

A person had developed within me who finally had some substance and belief in himself. Learning to adapt to many given situations in the past was the key to my success, as obstacles were hurled my way on a regular basis.

My life was changing fast and Liza sounded so happy about my job when we'd talk on the phone. We made plans for her to come and visit for a few months, which would give us the opportunity to get to know each other better. The phone calls and letters were nice, but we needed and wanted to be together. E-mail had not been introduced so I composed love letters with paper and pen.

After four months apart, Liza flew to the States. She appeared to like Milwaukee and quickly decided she wanted to move there. She was wonderful—full of questions, and still full of energy.

We drove to Chicago and around Wisconsin, which she enjoyed. During most days, I'd go to work, and Liza became a bit lonely. I offered suggestions on a number of things she could do, including coming with me some days. She liked the idea of being together, so she traveled with me from account to account, staying in the car and listening to music.

At lunch, I introduced her to new foods. Chinese food and pizza were familiar to her, so we ventured to other ethnic and specialty restaurants. Brats and burgers were a treat for her.

"Aren't you going to want to do more than hang out in the car?" I asked. "Do you have any interests you'd like to pursue? I'd be happy to help you."

"I'm happy just being with you, Scotty. That's all I need. Does that make me strange?"

"Not at all, Liza; I just don't want you becoming bored. How about meeting people? Have you had any success? I can have some of my friends' wives introduce you to more women if you'd like."

Whenever I brought this up she'd say, "I'm fine," give me a big smile and wave her hand like it was no big deal.

When she stayed home, Liza watched TV, made dinner and read romance novels. Sometimes, she'd venture out on her own to discover the neighborhood or do some shopping. Now cold and wintery out, we bought her a heavy coat, gloves, boots and some clothes to keep her warm. I asked, "Is the warmer weather in Israel whispering in your ear?" as we made our way from the frozen sidewalks of Milwaukee to my apartment.

"Yes, just a little," she said with a grin, "but the snow is so beautiful."

Being outgoing and fluent in English, Liza had little trouble making her way around our neighborhood stores. I'd come home to stories of walks she had taken and the shops she went to visit. I smiled, listening as she described her day.

By now my friends had met her and offered their opinions, as people will do whether or not you ask them. Some were just curious; others took an instant liking to her. A few were concerned and asked me to take my time, perhaps seeing something that my partial blindness from being in love did not.

Love is wonderful. Those emotions, pumping hormones, and desire are some of the finest feelings we humans can have. It drives some to murder and others to great personal sacrifice. Liza and I were taking a chance on love and putting ourselves out there, knowing that it can be the finest thing in the world.

It can also blow up in your face.

Our relationship felt wonderful, yet I sensed uneasiness in her. While I couldn't put my finger on it, I could see that she wasn't adapting to Milwaukee as she and I had hoped. We discussed this, and she assured me over and over again that being with me was all that mattered to her. Hearing that made me feel wonderful.

The topic of living in Israel did come up. We had agreed that, if we were to marry, better opportunities could be had in the States. Israel's economy continued to struggle and many people were leaving to find better paying jobs outside the country. Liza assured me that she would find work in Milwaukee and visit home every year or two. "I can live on a mattress if I have to. I just want to be with you and away from Israel. I love my family, but there's nothing there for me. I like to raise children here too, if we get married."

Another month went by and I became increasingly concerned because she showed little desire to acclimate to her new life. I tried to find things that would interest her, introduced her to more people and asked if I could help her find a job. She had excuses for not looking for work. "It's not easy and I don't want to just settle, Scotty."

"Can I help you more? I don't want you to become bored with Milwaukee or me. You could get certified as a massage therapist. This is what you wanted to do when we met in Israel."

"How about if I just ride around with you and hang out while you sell? You're doing so well and I don't want to be home alone every day."

It just wasn't feeling right, and I knew it deep down. I decided that it would be necessary for her to go home and take some time to think. Neither of us was as happy as we had hoped, yet we didn't know exactly why. Wanting a different outcome, but not sure what to do, Liza flew back to Israel.

I missed her but knew she had to decide what she really wanted for her life. She seemed lost and had trouble finding her way. I wanted us to be happy together. I didn't want her miserable and searching for who knows what while living in Milwaukee.

We talked and sent letters to keep the relationship strong, but I sensed that things were not going to work out as we had hoped. Distance and time had gotten in the way. Sadly, we stopped talking and writing after three months.

◆ ◆ ◆

CHAPTER 13

COME MARRY ME, PLEASE

◆ ◆ ◆

I WENT OUT on a few dates to ease my loneliness. It helped, but no sparks flew. After several months passed, I received a call from my friend Patty, the stepmother to my godson Sean. She had been in touch with Liza.

"Scotty, I think Liza wants to marry you, but she is afraid she's upset you too much. Why don't you write her or give her a call?"

Happy to hear this and dreaming of a future with Liza, I was on the phone to her the next day. I had always wanted to marry someone different and the thought of marrying someone who was from another country appealed to me a lot. We had connected in a wonderful way and I wanted to be with her and grow as a couple. *Exotic, full of energy,* and *intriguing* worked for me. Perhaps because my life with women and relationships had not always been so great, I figured that I might as well do something completely different than I had in the past, hoping for a lifetime of love, passion and new experiences.

Liza shared her thoughts and offered up a plan after we reconnected: come to Israel to marry me and we will move to the States after the wedding. "Are you sure that you can live so far from home, Liza?" I asked. "Last time you were here, you had a difficult time finding happiness. What's changed, my love?"

"I have. I want to be with you and you are allowing me to get married back home. That means so much to me and I love you for that. I will find work in Milwaukee and I promise to make a beautiful home for us."

I searched my soul, talked to friends and family, and quickly decided that we could fix any issues between us. A few people whose opinions I trusted advised against it, while others were happy about my decision. Thrilled that I agreed, Liza said that she would begin making the arrangements in the quaint seaside town of Tiberius. All I had to do was show up.

The date was set for July 22, 1986. After a quick phone call to my sister, she agreed to go with me, which made me very happy. "I'd like to visit the West Bank, Jerusalem and perhaps Tel Aviv if we have time," she said. "Do you think her family will be okay with my staying in their home?"

"Of course they will. We are welcome there with open arms. They're a warm group that love to laugh, argue, and laugh some more."

Carole and I were met in Tel Aviv by Liza and several family members. We drove back to her house and talked for a while until jetlag set in.

We slept for ten hours and awoke to a beautiful day that had me smiling. I was in love and being treated like family.

Carole, Liza, and I traveled to the West Bank and Jerusalem at my sister's request. Once again, Jerusalem cast a wonderful spell on me. Smiles were abundant among the shopkeepers. Her usual charming and caring self, Carole spoke to Arabs to get some personal opinions on the conflicts and wars. People were open with their thoughts and passionate about different solutions.

We spent the next few days getting to know all of her family. I found myself growing closer to them with every passing hour. They liked the fact that I was from America, but tried to be 'cool' about it. I liked that they were not from the States. Her brothers had taken to me and had many questions about life in America. "Hey," one asked, "tell us about America, your music and, your lovely women." s

Then Liza's father, Joseph, entered the room and sat in his chair. I could tell just by looking at him that he had lived and seen a lot. The undisputed king of the castle and a bit of a charmer himself, he was fluent in four languages, which made communicating easy. I learned from Liza's siblings that their mother, Rachel, was a saint raising seven children and dealing with her oftentimes overbearing husband. Joseph liked to sit in "his chair" with his shirt off barking orders to whoever crossed his path. He and Liza's mother gave me their blessing and a few days later we were husband and wife.

We were married in a large hall that also served as the town's bomb shelter. The rabbi who performed our ceremony, dressed all in black with a long salt-and-pepper beard, had a kind smile. He didn't speak a lick of English, so I had little idea as to what he or anyone else was saying. I could have been agreeing to give up every second organ in my body, for all I knew.

We made promises and signed papers and then I crushed the glass that her brothers placed before me with my right foot.

We had a very Jewish wedding with the lifting of the groom on the chair and an overabundance of food and desserts.

We ate deliciously prepared foods, and many of the 130 attendees danced for hours to Mideastern and European music. Liza has a large extended family, many of whom came to celebrate. I met them all and received many kisses on both cheeks. Things began to settle down around midnight and Liza and I made a quiet exit to our hotel room.

The next morning we spoke more about kids, and Liza made it clear that she wanted to be a mother. I told her that I wanted to wait a while until we were settled. Apparently okay with that, she listened as I also explained that we needed to get her a job and make sure she felt comfortable in her new home. She hugged me. "I love you so much. How long do you think we should wait to have kids? "

"Well, we should wait a year or two and make sure we have a solid foundation before we become parents." I could tell she wasn't thrilled about that, but I knew that it would be better for us to wait.

We spent three more days with my new family. Then, the time came to say good-bye. Carole, Liza, and I flew back to the States after a wonderful time in Israel.

Liza brought several large suitcases filled with most of her earthly belongings. I felt for her, and we often discussed how she might make the successful transition to living so far from home. "Don't worry, I'm going to be fine," she said. Her confidence, coupled with her accent and cuteness, made it easy to believe that this adult of 27 years had her feet firmly planted on this earth.

We arrived at our apartment and threw our things in a spare

KIDJACKED ◆ A FATHER'S STORY

room, which doubled as my office. Carole headed back to her home in L.A.

It wasn't long before we began looking for a house. We were fortunate to have enough for a down payment, and within two weeks we made an offer on a beautiful three-bedroom English Tudor in Whitefish Bay, ten minutes north of Milwaukee.

Thrilled to own a piece of the rock, we moved in and added our personal touches. We bought and painted furniture to fill the place up a bit and, of course, put in new carpet. We went out with friends for dinner or had them over to our house. I did my best trying to keep up with her desire to go dancing and improved a bit as we went to some of the best nightclubs. I could tell that she liked her new life, and I loved the way she danced and smiled.

Four months had passed since our marriage. We decided to take a trip to Florida, which Liza loved in part because of the warm weather and also because she began to get to know Eve, my grandmother. Liza adored her and Eve liked her as well. We took long walks at night holding hands. I told her stories of some of my awkward times in high school and she laughed hard. Before heading home, my grandmother confided in me, "Sweetheart, I've never met a person who has so many opinions on so many subjects. She believes that she knows more than anyone else and is always right."

I had to listen to this 80-year-old woman because she was very wise, gentle, and always honest. I hugged her, gave her a kiss, and whispered in her ear, "Thank you nanny. I love you."

◆ ◆ ◆

I had dozed off when the person in the middle seat asked for me to let her pass by to use the bathroom. I got up, walked to the back of the plane, and asked for a Pepsi and some pretzels. I eavesdropped on conversations while gazing out the little round window. I looked at my Timex: almost nine hours in the air. Gazing out the jet's rear window into the black sky I continued accessing the haphazard events that led to the Kidjacking of Jonathan and Alexandra.

◆◆◆

Liza began looking for work and now had a license in massage therapy from Israel. She scoured newspapers and called hair salons that offered massage to their clients. She also traveled to people's homes with her massage table and did well. She began making beaded jewelry. I went shopping with her and help pick out new colors for her creations. I even tried to make some, but they always fell apart. I continued working and earning a nice income while improving my sales skills.

Liza had wanted children, as did I. We had agreed to wait a while so that we could spend time with each other before becoming parents. A big move far from home for Liza and a marriage proved to be plenty for both of us to wrap our arms around, so kids could wait.

Or could they?

◆◆◆

CHAPTER 14
I'VE GOT SOMETHING TO TELL YOU

◆◆◆

SIGNS PRESENTED THEMSELVES to me in the first month of our marriage. Most days, Liza would ask me when we were going to start a family. She remained relentless, but I believed that we needed more time together. Fond of telling "white lies" when it benefited her, this behavior became a regular occurrence. At first, I tried to blow it off as nerves or anxiety, but I noticed a pattern. One night at dinner I asked her why she was not completely truthful with me. "Aw, come on, Scotty, a woman has to have some secrets to keep things spicy."

"I'm not talking secrets, my love. I'm talking about not being truthful with me. Are you afraid of how I will react? I need you to always be honest. Will you do that please?"

"I'm not afraid of anyone. I will try not to tell white lies anymore. There, are you happy now?"

"I am if you are being honest," I said with a smile.

She smiled back and hit me on my arm. "Yes, of course I am."

After six months since saying "I do" in Hebrew, Liza worked

up the nerve to spring the news on me. She was pregnant! I know that I should have been excited, but how in the world could this happen? She used a diaphragm. I would even remind her just to make sure. I wanted kids when we both were ready. The future mother of my child had betrayed me, big time.

It appeared that the last few "sessions," as Liza liked to refer to them, were minus one very important sperm trapper. This didn't happen by accident. It appeared to me to be calculated since who knows when, even though I was assured "it" was in.

I couldn't believe that she had done such a thing. When I asked why she did this to us, Liza replied, "It is my body and I can do what I want. Scott, the women have to do all the work so why should I not decide?" She smiled. "Come on, you'll be a great father and I'll be an even better mother."

These were her exact words to her now stunned husband who stared at her, motionless. After 30 seconds, I asked what anyone might ask, "Why would you do such a thing? We're supposed to be a team and make these important decisions as a couple."

Liza went on to tell me that she wanted children badly and how it was the woman's decision as to when and how many. She would take care of everything and I could just sit back and relax. Hmm. I thought about this tempting proposition for about three seconds.

Fuming, I left the room and headed out the door to Bobby's house for some much-needed consoling. He told me that she had expressed her desire to have children to him soon after we returned from the wedding. Bobby had warned me when he met Liza during her first visit to Milwaukee, "Just be careful. Liza is up to something, I just don't know what it is," he'd said.

"Can you believe this is happening?"

He just shrugged. "Keep your eyes on her, man."

Sandy, Bobby's wife and my good friend, interjected, "Liza is in it for herself, Scott. I can tell by some conversations we had, but until now I never thought she'd pull something like this. She has mentioned to me that she wanted children several times. I just thought it was two women sharing their feelings. She also said that she wanted to move to Israel with you and them on more than one occasion."

Wanting to take charge of my adulthood, I chose my path and felt good about important decisions I had made. I believed in us and was excited to begin our life together.

Enter Liza, my wife, friend, and now liar. I now found myself in a tough position, with few options that appealed to me. This was not the way I envisioned finding out I would be a dad. I wanted to be a partner in the decision, not simply the "tool."

When I came home, Liza had been crying and noticeably upset. I felt bad too and did not know what to say. She apologized as if it was a small mistake, but I wasn't buying it. She explained, "Middle Eastern women raise the children and are in charge of the home. It is the man's job to make the money."

"Christ Liza, what happened to my independent woman? I'm not buying your excuse either. This is your dream, not ours. Not all women from the Middle East want to have a family and even fewer would go about it in the way you did." Bobby's family came from Palestine and he and his wife discussed these things before having their son.

Was I missing something here? In a marriage where two people depend on each other, did her independence trump all?

A month passed. Liza was still without a job and with child.

Several tense discussions took place where I made it crystal clear that I felt betrayed and that our young marriage was in jeopardy. Liza pleaded with me to understand. The issue for me would be accepting it and moving on because our marriage was shaky, with lies as the root of the problem. A week later, while driving home, I made up my mind.

I came home from work one day and told Liza that we would become parents in eight months. She smiled, cried, smiled some more, and gave me a huge hug. I had made the decision that this would not break us apart, and had come to terms on the whole *being a father* front. I asked her to always be honest with me in the future and she happily agreed. I chose to take her at her word. I had done what I thought was best. It was time to look forward because we had a kid on the way.

Liza's belly continued to grow. She had regular checkups to make sure the two of them were well. One day when we were discussing names, Liza looked to the sky. "If it is a boy, I'd like to name him Sunshine, Sunny for short."

I suggested we give the child a name that works well in both Hebrew and English. She mentioned Yonatan (Yo-na-tan), which meant Jonathan in English. Yoni equaled Johnny, so there it was.

The next day, I called my brother. "Hey, Bruce, we picked out a baby name. His name will be Jonathan; the doctor informed us that we're having a son. I will not get into the name she wanted for a girl because it is not relevant... OK, Moonbeam."

"I'm happy you were able to work things out, Scotty. I'm going to be an uncle! So Sunshine is out," he said, laughing.

"I'm just happy that he is looking healthy in her tummy, big brother. We are doing better, but she's continuing to tilt stories to suit her fancy. These lies about where she goes and getting a job and what she really wants from life are troubling. I don't really know her well enough and she refuses to be completely open. That frightens me."

"Well, just keep an eye on her and try to find more things to occupy her time. Has she made any friends?"

"Yes and no. She makes them, but they never last. Maybe she just needs to click with the right people. I've even tapped into an Israeli group in Milwaukee that we spend time with, but she appears to be a bit of an outsider to them."

We spoke more, promising to talk again soon.

My work continued to go well. Liza focused her attention on making our home ready as she entered her third trimester. We had cut back on smoking to about two cigarettes a day.

I kept my eyes and ears open for any more lies.

Jonathan Lesnick was born on June 18, 1987 at three in the morning. Our lives changed big time as this colicky little man made his presence known immediately. Blonde curls and a cute laugh were his other early trademarks. He began crawling quickly and I had to watch him closely at all times. I fell in love with him in an instant, and watched as our three lives changed on a daily basis.

I began reading stories and singing to him. I noticed he liked the sound of music and the beat of drums. We'd lie on the den floor and I'd stand him up to dance to the tunes. He'd laugh and plop onto my belly.

Liza often told me how much she enjoyed being a mother. She'd also tell me how difficult she had it every day, and I understood to a point. Raising children is hard, but she wanted this for her life and began to realize all of the work and lack of sleep that comes with the honor of being a parent. I'd come home early sometimes to catch them napping. It was such a sweet sight. We took the stroller out for long walks, just the three of us. We sang songs in English and Hebrew and invented some new words as we moved slowly from park to park. I held Jonathan's hands as he slid down slides and played on the merry-go-round. Sometimes, we brought food and a blanket and had picnics.

Liza continued adapting to the roles of wife and mother as well as she could, and I learned the roles of husband and father and enjoyed both.

I knew through conversations with her and others (she would talk to anyone who listened) that she was still not as happy as she'd hoped. The largest issue remained the fact that she missed her home, and that she wanted to raise our family in Tiberius. The large family she had left in Israel was now pulling her back home emotionally, while she attempted to deal with internal problems that I never knew existed. I wondered if she was ever really satisfied and happy in her life. She remained convinced that she had it harder than anyone else did.

At the same time, Liza would express her happiness with me and our relationship every day. "I'm so lucky to have you, Scotty," was commonly sent my way with a smile and a kiss. I felt the same and told her that. My love and commitment grew stronger.

Israel was far away and the people she had seen on most days of her life were no longer a few blocks away. She made some friends, but I noticed a continuing pattern developing. These friends simply didn't last long.

◆◆◆

Hungry after flying for ten hours, I ate my breakfast, had several cups of coffee and some snacks I had stuffed in my backpack. I took the warm towel the flight attendant handed me as I pass her my tray. I wiped my face in lieu of a shower and tried to make sure I covered every possible angle one more time before landing. I drifted back to our children.

◆◆◆

I believed that Liza's openness and willingness to talk to anyone was the key to her happiness. Yet, inside her were demons that she either didn't recognize or simply thought of as normal. Others took notice of her personality, and some did not like what they saw or heard. Liza had no filter when it came to dialogue and thoughts, thus the most outrageous things would come from her mouth. At first, I enjoyed her ability to speak her mind so openly; later, I actually grew embarrassed when we were among people. This wasn't the feeling one wants to have as it pertains to their spouse, and I struggled to make sense of it. She continued telling me and anyone else who'd listen that she still hadn't found true happiness in Milwaukee.

"We need to be in Israel, Scotty. I can't breathe here. Take me home!" she'd yell.

Having grown up in the "loud voice" home, I tended to date women who were able to express themselves at a lower decibel level than a scream. The only way I could get a word in when Liza became upset was to yell louder. I could, but it felt out of character. I asked her if we could discuss things in a normal tone, and she said she'd try. It never happened; she claimed it was due to her background. Her white lies continued.

When Jonathan turned a year old, Liza took a trip back to Israel with our son while I stayed to work and take care of the house. Almost relentless in her desire to go, I was reluctant to agree because I needed our bond as a family to grow. When the topic of flying overseas came up, I told her that I thought we needed to continue working on our relationship.

I missed them both, but I really missed our boy. He and I had formed a tight bond and were always happy together. I wanted to play peek-a-boo and fly him around the house like a plane. I missed reading books to him as his little hands helped turn the pages. We laughed so hard when he would turn a page too quickly as if to say to me, 'Hey Dad, reading can be fun, too!'

I picked them up in Chicago after a month and a half away and was so happy to have them back. The empty house had been lonely, and I was ready for the three of us to have fun.

Shortly after recovering from jetlag, Liza began asking me to move to Israel. This continued often after they had returned home, and she was relentless. "Scott, if you love me, you will move to Israel. I want to be there and know I can make you happy."

"Don't you remember asking me to get married in Tiberius? You said that you'd move to the States and live here as we build our lives together. I asked many times if this was really what you wanted to make sure, for everyone's sake, that this exact topic did not interfere with our marriage. You assured me on many occasions that you were fine with this and even said that you were looking forward to it."

"Ya, ya, I know I said that, but I changed my mind and want

to live there. Is this so wrong, Scott? My family is there and so is my life. What am I supposed to do?"

"I kind of thought your life was here now. We have a sweet young boy, a home, and my work is here in Milwaukee," I said sadly.

No jobs awaited us there, only her family, who shared with me on numerous occasions the miserable employment outlook in Israel. "We need to be where we can make a living. We agreed that Milwaukee would be our home. I can't make money there at this time, even your family has told me so," I said.

As the months went on, she never let up and became even more focused. We took short vacations to Northern Wisconsin and Chicago. I tried to help her as best as I could, but her mind was made up. Israel was where she wanted us to live, and continuing to debate the pros and cons did little to dissuade her.

Jonathan continued to make me smile. We were now playing catch with a Nerf football every day. He'd run to me and toss it at my body. He'd burst out laughing as I'd fall to the ground from the power of his throw.

Liza and I discussed having another child, but I didn't feel that we were ready. So why on earth did we continue to make love without any protection? Perhaps it was a weak moment on my part, which turned out wonderfully.

Liza begged me to allow her to go home and be with her mother when she was eight months pregnant with our daughter. I hesitated because I so much wanted to be there for the birth. Through eight months of pregnancy, I had help fill her requests for food at strange hours, and consoled her as she dealt with aches, pains, and morning sickness, but Liza insisted on giving birth in Israel. I gave in and let her go.

I had booked a ticket to be with my family and simply guessed at the birth date. I missed by two days welcoming our daughter into the world.

I kept thinking about our family dynamics. I thought the order of a family was a mother and father and children first and her family in Israel second.

Liza must have been thinking too, only her thoughts revolved around her mother and father and our children first, which left me alone again to work and long for them.

Having our daughter in Israel gave me another sign that things weren't right. Though I had reluctantly agreed that she could go home for the birth, deep down I felt I should have insisted that she have our baby in Milwaukee with the pediatrician we knew and my being there for support. I couldn't go over there for a month and a half and miss work. Maybe I would one day, but we needed my income to pay the bills.

I landed once again in Tel Aviv to great cheers and adulation from the passengers as they showed their happiness for touching down in the Holy Land. I rented a car and drove to the hospital in Tiberius. The jetlag was no match for not seeing my wife and children for five weeks. Then, I saw her for the first time. Alexandra (Ally) was born on June 21, 1989 in Tiberius, Israel with fiery red curly hair.

I gave Jonathan a big hug. He wouldn't let me go. I felt such warmth as I held him in my arms. I made my way over to Liza to give her a kiss and hug. She had a little trouble delivering our daughter but felt better and would be ready to leave the hospital the next morning.

Our lives were not stable enough to have a second child, but I was very happy we did. I was in love with these two kids and dedicated to my family in every way.

Ally was next to her mother in a crib with a blanket loosely wrapped around her. I instantly noticed her abundant red curls. What a beautiful little girl, I thought, as I smiled and gazed at her. Her brother seemed to like having a baby sister. I held him in my arms and then placed him on the bed next to his mother. I had a daughter to hug.

Five days later the four of us headed back to Milwaukee.

Once back home with the kids, Liza enjoyed showing off her two angels to anyone she could. They became her identity.

I went back to work. Ally and I formed a close bond. She would crawl around the house looking for me if I wasn't in sight.

I was happy at home and at work, but Liza still felt like a caged tiger. She often told the little ones that we were going to move to Israel and made it sound so wonderful. To them it did, and so began her campaign of building up Mommy and breaking down Daddy. She'd tell them how much she loved them and how much she needed them. This occurred several times a day, every day, in front of anyone. She didn't let up, and was dubbed "Smother Mother" by one of our neighbors. Liza continued to tell the children that they'd soon be living in Israel.

My Hebrew improved. She constantly spoke it to the kids because she wanted them to be fluent. I had no problem with that as long as I knew what was going on. I heard enough words that led me to the conclusion that she was now telling them that Daddy won't let them go to Israel. Jonathan started asking, "Dad, why can't we go home with Mom? We want to be in Israel. This is not our home."

Keeping a confident outward appearance, I gently told him that Milwaukee was where we live and where I work. However, the damage had been done and Liza started making me appear as the bad guy to our children to further push her agenda.

I didn't trust her to say the right things to them anymore. Later, I learned my mistrust was accurate because Liza resorted to her native tongue when telling things to the kids she did not want me to understand. Naïvely believing that I had little idea as to what was being said, Liza went about this behavior every day.

One day I'd had enough. I told Liza that I understood everything she said to our children in Hebrew. (I did not; a white lie on my part, but she bought it). She changed her times of manipulation to coincide with my work schedule. Sadly, her clever but unhealthy move hurt our children and our marriage once again.

Had I not done my part as a husband, father, and provider? Why undermine me and begin a long process of messing with our little ones' minds and hearts? I began to realize that she had no desire to control herself or think about anyone else *but* herself.

◆ ◆ ◆

The 13 hour flight was without event. I had attempted to sleep for a few hours, but couldn't. Beside myself with fear, self doubt, and rage at the position I was in, I held out my hand to check my nerves: it was trembling. I focused on my breathing while telling myself that everything would work out fine. I knew that there were several possible endings to my mission. Only one scenario would be acceptable to me. I tried to stay strong and focused on flying home with the kids as our plane touched down in Tel Aviv, Israel.

As always, we landed to plenty of cheering and applause as we prepared to deplane, but I felt none of their happiness this time around. In fact, as I sat looking down at the floor, I loathed their show of joy.

I passed through customs looking for any sign of my family. Liza said she would be waiting with a car to shuttle us back to her home.

All at once I saw them. Ally was in Liza's arms and Jonathan stood clutching her leg. They had grown a bit and both looked breathtaking to my eyes. Dressed in shorts and tee shirts with Hebrew writing on them, they smiled and I smiled and the four of us hugged. It felt fantastic holding my children, and I told them all how much I missed and loved them. Red and brown curls waved in the air. Our son was a bit distant, which I knew would happen. Sadly, his mother had pumped him so full of thoughts, he had little time to be a kid. We hugged some more and then headed to the car with one of her brothers who had accompanied them to the airport.

Jonathan said in his little voice, "Dad, are you really moving to Israel? That's great, Dad. Mom isn't sure and we don't want to go back. You can't make us go back, can you?"

That placed me squarely in a position where I had to decide whether or not to lie to my son for his, Ally's, and my sake. I lied.

Making sure Liza could hear me, I said, "Sweetheart, we're going to live wherever Mommy wants."

Liza said, "Scotty, you look good. We've missed you."

The perfect opportunity presented itself. Stopping in front of our children I picked their mother up and gave her a hug that lasted a full ten seconds. When I put her down, I gave her a kiss and said in Hebrew, "I love you and missed you so much."

I watched her face and saw her smile. The truth is that I wanted nothing more than to be as far away as possible from the person who so harmed our family, but I held back so I could attempt to implement my plan and not further traumatize our kids. Her brother watched, too, and I greeted him warmly with a smile and kisses on each cheek as if nothing had happened.

Although nearly impossible, I attempted to keep my anger and emotions in check. I had to use an enormous amount of self control and found myself cringing at the sound of her voice.

As we drove the winding roads to Tiberius, I listened to the kids' stories, breathing in every lost minute of the last eighteen weeks. They were happy playing with their cousins. Now two, Ally was speaking a lot thanks to a big brother who talked with her all the time.

Sitting on my lap in the back seat, Jonathan broke off from stories of their life to ask a question. "Daddy, why didn't you come to see us sooner? Have you been working too much?"

"Sweetheart, I'm so sorry I was gone for so long. I had to work hard for Mommy and you and Ally, but I missed you all so much." He accepted my answer and smiled.

Ally crawled into my arms as if to say, 'Daddy, don't leave us, please.'

Now holding one child on each knee with an arm around them, I instantly knew that I had done the right thing.

When we arrived at Liza's parents' home, her family greeted me with warmth and hugs along with coffee and food. With ten pairs of eyes on me, I pretended that I was playing a role on TV, refusing to break character.

I awoke the next morning after eleven hours of sound sleep. *I'm alive and unharmed*, I thought as I rolled out of bed. As my feet hit the floor both kids were up on the bed with books in their hands. They laughed as I tried to read them a *Sesame Street* story in Hebrew. Throwing my hands up in the air and smiling, I asked for a book in English. Ally gave me three books with lots of pictures. Thankfully, one was in English. We lay back on the bed, got under the covers, positioned the pillows just right, and I proceeded to read them a humorous story book by Shel Silverstein. I was in heaven. After 15 minutes of giggling they jumped off the bed and said, "Time to eat."

Liza's family milled about and I only heard Hebrew. My thoughts immediately turned to the kids, so I searched for them. They were in the TV room watching *Sesame Street* in Hebrew and eating breakfast. Seeing me, they turned and both opened their arms wide for a hug. I happily obliged, giving them two very long squeezes and then two more just for me. I just wanted to be next to them when...

In walked Joseph, Liza's father and alpha male of the family. He smiled and gave me a kiss on both cheeks. *Lucky me*, I thought as I smiled and sat down outside on their patio. The kids sat close by, as did most of her family. I tried so hard not to stare at them, showing my feelings of loss and the debilitating pain I had suffered.

Liza walked in with a cautious smile. I smiled back and left to brush my teeth. When I returned, she hugged me and said, "Good morning." We sat together next to the kids and talked. Immediately she asked me in front of our children, "Scott, are you serious about moving to Israel? I need to know because we have made a life here, and we're not going back."

"Yes, of course," I replied.

Ally jumped onto my lap. Her brother sat beside me listening.

The camera in my head continued rolling and this was a one-take, live production with no chance for editing. I didn't want to discuss things in front of the children, but Liza spoke her mind no matter who was present, so I had no choice but to continue the charade in front of them. I kept smiling at her, waiting for her next words to give me a clue for my next line.

"I'm not sure what to do. I want to work here and have more kids. I want you to be here too, but I think you might be mad at me for leaving like I did. People are giving me all kinds of advice, and I don't know what to do. I know the kids want to stay here, and I will find a job. I did what any mother would do, you know." Always direct, she asked in almost perfect English, "Scotty, are you mad with me? I did what I thought was best. America is not for me, and I need to be close to home and my mom. Did you meet anyone else?"

"I'd be lying if I didn't admit I was upset, Liza, but I thought about how much I love and need you and the children. Now I just want to be here. You were right. This is the place for us. However, with the economy, we might have to consider living in Tel Aviv to earn money. All that really matters is that we are together again, and I don't care if it is Africa, China, or Australia. Do you know how much gas costs here? Is food that much more expensive here than in the U.S.? Where do you think we should send the kids for school?"

As I continued asking questions, I could literally see the ice melting and her steel wall lowering. I continued, "I have made arrangements for us to move, with the Shaliah in Milwaukee, as I mentioned to you before. He helped me a lot and we are ready to put the papers through. I'd like to go over the paperwork with you when the time is right."

"I'm happy that you spoke to the Shaliah. It's important to fill out all of the paperwork properly if you plan on moving here. I have already looked into school for the kids and found a nice one close to my parents' home."

She answered my questions, and then the conversation turned to her.

While actually biting my tongue, I listened to her reasons for wanting to be in Israel while smiling to stop from blurting, "Hey, what about the kids? Look at what you have done! I should be home working and yet I am here. I want to hop on the next flight out of this place with the kids and never see you again." Yet, I managed to smile and stay composed as the cameras inside my head kept rolling. Her mother and two brothers entered the room. They kept silent, and I felt awkward now that we were not alone, so I changed the conversation.

I spoke to her mother while we snacked on pistachios. She too wanted Liza to stay in Israel. I offered a warm outward appearance, all the while continuing to assess my situation.

After half an hour I excused myself, took a shower and looked for my kids. Jonathan was on the patio playing with trucks. I sat on the ground and joined him.

"Daddy, I missed you. Will you stay here and not go home?"

"Well my love, Mommy and I have to talk about it. We love you and Ally so much and we will figure out where we'll all live. Don't worry," I said with a confident smile. "Everything will be fine. Let's play!"

We crashed the trucks into each other and made a lot of noise in the process. Hearing all of the laughter and commotion,

Ally ran out to get in on the action. Always the climber, she worked her way onto my shoulders and then my head.

"Up. Up," she said, so I stood up and flew her around the patio until I got dizzy.

◆ ◆ ◆

Later that afternoon while the kids were napping, I sat on the back patio with Liza's father eating watermelon. He spoke about Israel as a young man, his life when he first arrived and how much he loved his children. No one interrupted us, which was rare, as I remained quiet listening for direction. He gazed up at me after spitting out some seeds on the ground.

Not wearing a shirt, I could see that he was once a man of great natural strength. His intense eyes and deep stare intimidated me. Now in his late fifties, his hair and mustache were graying; he was heavy and moved at a slower pace. "Scotty, my son, I heard that you want to move here to raise the family, is this true?"

Having rehearsed my lines well, I stated, "Yes, Joseph. I want to live here because this is where my wife will be the happiest. The children will be fine wherever their parents are, you understand."

A slight smile came across his face. Could he see right through me? Was I busted and about to get busted up? I kept wondering what lies Liza had told him and how awful she made me look, still hoping to maintain my balance during what felt like an interrogation. "What are your plans for moving here? How long do you think it will take you? Perhaps I'll find a job for you in Tiberius, that way you and Liza and the children will be close to us."

"I have made arrangements with the Shaliah in Milwaukee, Joseph. We will be able to move in about two months after all the paperwork is approved and our belongings are shipped. We also have to sell our home, but it should move pretty quickly because it is in a desirable neighborhood and it is a strong seller's market. I'm ready to tell my company that I'll be leaving."

"And where in Israel do you want to live, Scotty?"

"I don't know for sure, Joseph. Liza and I have to decide on the best place for us to live and work. It might end up being Haifa or Tel Aviv. Perhaps you have some contacts that would be useful to me in those cities too. I could really use your help."

"I do. I know people all over the country, Jews and Arabs. Are you going to stay in sales or do you have another job you would like to do?"

"I am going to have to see what is available and how much it pays. I hope to buy a home here for us so Liza can have her massage business in one of the rooms."

So far so good from my vantage point. I was beginning to feel a little less knotted up inside—and that's when he blindsided me.

"Scotty, *if* Liza goes back to help you move, I want you to leave the children here with us. We will take care of them until you come back. Their grandmother and I will watch them and our children will help, too. I will miss them so much if they go again. It is too much for them to travel back and forth, and you and Liza will be busy packing. That will be best for everyone, I think. Don't worry my son, they'll have plenty of family keeping an eye on them. "

I never saw this coming. The ante was raised yet again and I was low on chips. I was left with no alternative but to go all in. Anything else would surely be a sign of weakness in his eyes.

My initial response was to panic, but with only seconds to respond and no clue as to what the appropriate answer would be, I gave it my best. For some reason, the location of where we were entered my mind as I grinned inside, hoping I had come up with the right answer.

I was in the Middle East, where a man and his family are sacred above all else. I'm not sure if it was my fifth gear, my gut, or just quick thinking. "Joseph, I appreciate the offer so much but the children belong with their parents, and I need Liza's help with this big move. We don't know exactly how long this will take and the kids are too young to spend long periods of time away from us. The separation would be too difficult for them. We will be back soon and celebrate our new lives together."

I stopped there, knowing that the next person who spoke would lose and I wasn't going to let it be me. My breath was shallow, and my heart raced as I sat awaiting his response.

Now reaching 100 degrees in the shade and looking me straight in the eye, this man from the Middle East who had the fate of my children in his hands understood a father's position in the home. "Scotty, my son, if that is your wish then it is okay with me. Please bring them home soon you know, because I will miss them very much. I want all of you here."

I had never dodged a closer bullet. I assumed he could see me hyperventilating and twisting my fingers underneath the patio table. We proceeded to hug, eat watermelon and drink tea. Having his blessing was one of the keys to my leaving quietly on the plane in four days with Alexandra, Jonathan, and hopefully the soon to be dethroned Queen.

That evening at dinner, everyone wanted to talk with me. All six brothers and sisters had specific questions, though not one mentioned a word about what Liza had done and its effect on our children. I began my rapid fire round in broken English mixed with some Hebrew.

Yahuda, the eldest of the seven, started the questioning. "Scotty, my man, when will you and Liza be moving here? We will miss Yoni and Ally too much. Have you thought about where you will live? How about an apartment in Tel Aviv? Tiberius doesn't have any jobs. Do you want me to come to America and help you get ready? You could show me around and we could have some fun."

Elana was next. "Scotty, my brother, I'm so happy you decided to move here! Do you want me to come and help you pack up the house? This will be a lot of work for Liza and I will miss your kids too much. You know you should leave Yoni and Ally here with me. I can take care of them for you. They can play with their cousins. They'll just be in the way when you are busy packing up the house."

I never entertained it, but thanked her just the same.

My mind raced as I went over the conversation with Joseph in my head while I answered their questions with a slight smile, maintaining strong eye contact with each of them.

Although Liza had not yet said that she was going to fly back with me, her father had given his blessing. I needed to continue to work on her and convince her of my love and my desire to move to Israel. I had planned so hard to get to this moment, and I still had plenty of work to do.

The following evening, I was halfway home with the kids in my mind when I asked Liza if she would like to go into town for dinner. She agreed. We had a pleasant meal and several drinks. Not much of a drinker myself, I decided I had to do this to loosen us both up. She confided in me. "I'm confused. You look so good and I want to be with you, but I'm not sure what to do. I probably hurt you, but I want to be here with my family."

"What else is confusing you?" I asked gently.

"I'm a good mother and I want more children. I know we agreed to only have two, but I love them so much. Do you want to have more children with me, Scott?"

"We could if you want, but I think we need to be settled here first. Look, Liza, I just want to be with you. I don't care how many more kids we have or where we live as long as we're together. I've had plenty of time to think about things, that's why I'm here."

Her face widened into a bright smile. Though she never apologized for her past mistakes and lies, she appeared ready to move forward with me, if only for the time being.

I would prefer to have my memory completely wiped clean after making my next move, but I did what I had to do to get back to the States with our children.

We rode a cab back to her parents' home where the kids were sleeping. I took Liza's hand and escorted her to our small bedroom for some private time together. I thought, *Hey, you're going to have to be smoother than you've ever been.* And I used every move that I could think of. I romanced, seduced, and massaged her body and ego. I also made damn sure that I was using birth control.

The next scene in my nightmarish trip showed Liza once and for all how much I cared. It seemed to work. Afterward, we stayed in bed, cuddled, and talked about the impending move as I held her in my arms. We whispered softly to each other.

"Scotty, do you really love me or are you just pretending? Don't mess with me. I'm a big girl. I can take it."

"Liza, if I did not love you with all of my heart do you think I'd fly all the way over here to see you? I need to be with you, and I am so happy just to be here. Remember when you told me you would not move back to the States, but I was welcome to come here to visit?"

"Yes, of course."

"I was hoping that you still had feelings for me after things did not go as you had hoped in Milwaukee. I'm to blame and I want to make it up to you. I wanted to see you and the kids so much, and I now understand what you meant when you said that you need to be with your family. They're a bit crazy, but they are wonderful, too."

She laughed. "They are crazy for sure. I hope that you really want to move here and are not just saying that for my sake. This is my home and we can try to make it yours, too, if you'd like. Are you mad at me?" she inquired, still constantly needing reassurance. "I kind of made some mistakes, but that's behind us now. I just know what's best for me and the kids."

"No, Liza, I'm beyond that, my love." I wondered if she understood my double meaning.

She never mentioned what she had done. Liza spoke hardly a word about Yoni and Ally, my two points of light that were now asleep in the next room. I never once mentioned the only two reasons that I had hopped on a jet in the first place: Alexandra and Jonathan Lesnick. As I saw it, I took one for the team of Yoni, Ally, and Dad. I felt cheap, but if it worked it would be worth it.

The next morning, Liza was all smiles and things looked peachy—or were they? She began asking me questions about our move, and I tried to be as nonchalant as possible. I was trying to decipher the conversation she was having with her mother when two of her brothers, Danny and Shimon, walked into the room. Both were cops and wanted me to join them at a shooting range about a half hour away in the hills. It was in an area against a mountain where people sometimes went for target practice, I was told. Internally, I questioned their motives. What was the target going to be? Me? Should I go? Christ, I almost wet my pants, because not going would surely have disappointed them and might mean something more, while going might mean death for me. Not one inch of my being wanted to step into a car with those fellas. They'd be packing, and I would be conveniently unarmed. They were well connected; I, a visitor from afar. Were they playing me the same as I was playing them? "Come on," her brother Danny yelled. "Let's hit the road, man. It will be too hot soon."

I studied them both, trying in vain to size them up, but noticed nothing in their faces or postures to give me a reason to say no.

Regrettably, we walked to their Renault, water jugs in hand as I climbed in the back. They asked me questions about the move and I said with much excitement and some apprehension, "We're moving here and Liza can tell you the specifics. I don't know which city because we will have to find jobs. I'm open to any suggestion you guys have."

The two of them spoke a few sentences in Hebrew that I did not understand, and I became even more nervous. I was literally in their backyard and a person could conceivably "get lost" forever if someone wanted it to happen. "English, please," I muttered from the back.

"Sorry about that, man. Forgot you were back there," Shimon said. "Look Scotty, I think it's best not to live in Tiberius. There are not many jobs. Tel Aviv and Haifa are your best bet for work my brother."

We arrived at the site, a noticeable amount of sweat pouring from my forehead. I stepped out of the car, unarmed, with two off-duty Israeli policemen who could strip apart an Uzi in the dark and put it back together in thirty seconds. I walked beside them toward a rocky hill one hundred yards ahead. I looked for possible escape routes and found none. Hoping that I could run faster than them, I realized that I couldn't outrun a bullet. As we approached the hill, Danny turned to me and said, "Here you go, man," and handed me a .45 caliber pistol. "Do you know how to shoot?"

As it turned out, the three of us simply went out to play that afternoon. Yet, I was worried every single second and kept a constant eye on each of them. They were great shots and both said I was a natural! It appeared as if I had dodged another bullet.

Liza sat on the patio waiting for us when we returned and asked to talk to me privately. I looked quickly for our kids and found them watching television. Never taking her eyes off the screen, Ally grabbed my hand and I tickled her tummy. I gave them each a kiss on the head and walked into the kitchen.

I poured a glass of cold water, walked into our bedroom and closed the door. With a piercing stare, she asked, "Did you really mean what you said about moving here? I need to know that you are not mad at me for what I did. I just wanted to be here, and I knew you would not want to live here. I want the children here, and I can't go back to America. I didn't know if you would ever talk to me again, and now you are here. I did what was best for me and the kids. We need to be here, can you see that, Scotty?"

Staring into her brown eyes, I gently took her hands and said, "Yes, my love, of course I meant what I said (*lie*). I've had a lot of time to think about this (*no lie*) and when I arrived here and saw you and the kids I knew what I wanted to do and where I wanted to be (*no lie—just not the place you think*). Four-and-a-half months were long enough for me to know what I want for my life. Are you upset with me about anything, Liza?"

"No, of course not, Scotty. You did nothing wrong. I just got confused and did what I thought was best for me the kids. You were wonderful to us, but you would not let me move home."

"I understand. My mind is made up, love," I smiled. "I can get a job and make money to support our family anywhere, so please don't be concerned with that. We have a lot of plans to make. Are you ready to dive into things?"

Hearing that made her smile and she followed that by giving me a big hug.

"Your father asked a good question. Which city do you think we should live in? Tel Aviv?"

"I love Tiberius, but it's small and there are not many jobs that pay well."

Not once since my arrival did Liza ask how I was doing over the last several months. Not once did she check to see how I was holding up without our children, who she decided to keep from their father. I saw big changes coming for Yoni and Ally with regard to where they'd be living. Thankfully, they had warmed up to their daddy quickly.

And then she said the words that cut through all of the legal red tape I was facing. Without these words, I had little chance of being a full-time father to my children.

"Scotty, I will fly back with you and the kids in a few days with the return tickets I have. Are you sure this is what you want?"

I sat next to her both shocked and thrilled that my plan had worked so well to this point.

"For me, this is the best because we will all be together and that is what a family is all about." With a final deep breath and fingers crossed, I asked, "Are you happy with us and the direction we are headed, Liza?"

She was and, lucky for me, had too much joy at that moment to gut check her soon-to-be-ex-husband's motives. I was in! I could not believe what had just happened. Everyone had grilled me until I was "well done" and I had surprisingly passed every test.

Well, almost everyone.

Liza's father almost put an end to my plan with his kind offer to keep an eye on the little ones, but I was moving forward just as fast as things had been crawling months before. Unfortunately for me, I didn't realize I'd have one more test to pass.

Liza's youngest sister is Simona. Her husband's name is Yitzhak, a nice guy who works with athletes as a shiatsu and massage therapist. A well-built man with glasses, he was fluent enough in English for us to talk with my basic Hebrew as backup.

The day before we were to fly back home to Milwaukee, Yitzhak asked to take a walk with me. I liked him and agreed. We hit the rolling streets and headed to a park about a half-mile from the house. Along our walk, I noticed his short black hair and strong features and asked where his parents were from. "Yemen. Have you ever been there?"

"Nope. How about you?"

"Not me either."

We continued to feel each other out, talking about America and the visit he made there for business. Israelis are no-bullshit people and ask point-blank questions that many Westerners are not comfortable doing. I asked him why this was so. He explained to me that the people don't always know what is going to happen day to day because of the area and its many conflicts. "Look, we don't feel we always have time to slowly ask our questions, so we tend to get to the point right away."

Liza had echoed the same sentiment to me in Eilat.

Once at the park we sat down. Wasting no time he looked me straight in the eye. "Scott, I know what you are doing. You're not coming back here with Liza and the children, are you?"

Meeting his strong gaze I replied, "Of course I am, Yitzhak."

We both smiled and assessed the situation. I waited for him to speak. "Why would you come back here? Life is not easy in Israel. I've traveled to the U.S. and like it very much. There is much opportunity in your country, not so much in mine."

Not sure what he was getting at and trusting no one, I kept my story the same as I had with Joseph. "This is where Liza wants to be and I want to be with her. It's that simple. Look, I have a family to think of and it's my job to look out for them."

The last thing I needed at this point was any more conflict or drama. I stood firm on my shaky ground, wondering what he was trying to accomplish. He gave me a crooked smile that said, "I'm on to you man." He probably was.

"I'm not sure what you're referring to," I continued. "People immigrate to Israel from all over the world, each having their own reasons for doing so. I'm no different."

He didn't reply, instead suggesting that we head back to the house.

I don't know if he mentioned his feelings to anyone. I like to think that he felt for my predicament as a man and as a father, and that he didn't approve of Liza's actions.

Liza opened the door to their home with tears in her eyes and her mother beside her. I received a hug from her mother and some from other family members as well. Mama said to me in her sweet, broken English, "Scotty, I love you. You are my son."

It was difficult to hear because she was a kind woman so I smiled and said, "I love you, too." I remained cautious, amazed and mentally and emotionally exhausted. My months of planning and performance had taken a toll on me. Liza smiled, having just finished playing backgammon with her sister. "You look tired."

"I am. It's siesta time."

I went to take a nap with the kids. Of course, we played and wrestled for a while because their dad needed it. They did as well. We had a pillow fight and they both piled pillows on me and jumped on top. I got in a few harmless licks to their faces with the pillows and then we nodded off.

I woke up first and decided to stay in bed and rest a while longer. I began to think.

I had nearly lost my children forever, and not a single person in this large family cared enough to ask me how I was doing. They wanted me to fold to Liza's demands, be nice and give everyone some peace. No one mentioned that Liza made a horrible mistake, and I realized that it was another sign that we were from different worlds and her family were enablers, at the very least. I made my way over the kids and out of the bedroom, closing the door behind me. I proceeded to call the airlines.

I waited on hold while the music played. Except for Yiztack, no one in her family had never been to the States and knew precious little about me. I suppose they just wanted everyone together in the small city so there would be four more people to get on the nerves of this large family. Fighting and arguing was normal for them and I could handle myself well, but any future battles would hopefully take place on my home turf.

My strategy all along was to go through Liza and not around her. It had finally taken shape after months of painstaking planning and agonizing nights spent alone.

Just as I had hoped, Liza had to agree to walk on a plane with our kids in tow, without kicking and screaming. There was no law requiring her to do so, a fact that haunted me every waking moment.

◆ ◆ ◆

CHAPTER 15

HOME AGAIN

◆ ◆ ◆

THE NEXT DAY we headed to Tel Aviv in three cars. I made sure my loves, Yoni and Ally, were in my vehicle.

As we pulled up to the El Al gate outside Ben Gurion International Airport, I had to remind myself that the internal joy I felt would have wait to show itself until we were over U.S. airspace. I had never been this nervous in all my life. I never took my eyes off of the little ones as we made our way inside. The airport appeared as I had left it one week ago, full of travelers, soldiers, and this time, my children.

Had I really pulled this off? I kept wondering. *Am I about to get on a jet heading back to the States with both of the kids?*

Liza and her parents were off to the side arguing about something, but I could not follow the discussion. I feared the worst and pictured everyone, including the children, climbing back into the cars and heading back to Tiberius. Forcing myself to remain calm, I took our children by the hand and walked over with a gentle smile.

I felt enormously relieved when I saw them begin to hug and kiss. I held tightly to my little ones' hands. We said our good-byes to Liza's family and walked to the ticket counter.

It was crowded and pushy. Some people appeared to have their life's belongings with them. We all had reserved seats, yet you'd think it was the last flight out of the country for months. We checked in and answered the multiple security questions. Still beside myself with both joy and apprehension, I took four boarding passes from the ticket agent. I knew I'd probably never be back in this country, and I didn't care. I said good-bye to the men and women carrying machine guns and wished them peace.

I had become attached to Liza's family. I knew I would miss them, but they listened to Liza's stories and lies and had sided with her. Perhaps they should have, as she was family. Perhaps I should have taken time off of work, flown over to try to retrieve my children, and miraculously pulled it off!

The doors of the jet slammed shut with a force that seemed to punctuate just how I felt at that moment. I sat across from the kids and Liza. Ally was looking out the window and Jonathan sat in the aisle seat. As we taxied down the runway, I put my hand out for his and he grabbed mine. We exchanged smiles and I sent him a wink. Clueless of what his father had just done on their behalf, my two points of light were heading home and I was sitting right next to them.

Off we went, higher and farther away, and I beamed from ear to ear. The desire to stand up and scream, *"YES! I DID IT"* while doing some crazy dance of joy was almost unbearable.

Many had told me that this day would never happen. "Please don't get your hopes up too much because you'll be in for a nasty fall," some had said. When I asked what they would do if this horrible scenario had beset them, many had no idea. Yet there I sat, on an airplane with my kids and Liza heading to America.

The long flight home gave me plenty of time to reflect back to day one in June when I had called to wish them all a happy birthday. Now, so tired and overjoyed as we continued heading west, I wanted to cry like a baby. I somehow kept my composure.

Several times each hour I glanced over to my right, giving myself an internal pinch as I made sure both kids were still there. I was proud and happy as ever that I had managed to figure this one out and see it through. Reunited with the two people who mattered most to me, I planned on never letting this happen again.

Friends and loved ones back home had not heard from me since I had landed in Tel Aviv. No one knew what had transpired, and I had a great story of success against some huge odds to share with them.

We landed in Chicago around noon to rain and cool fall weather. I asked myself if this was a sign of a personal storm brewing on the horizon, but mostly I just wanted to make it through passport control, pick up our luggage and drive the ninety minutes north to Milwaukee.

The next morning, I checked on the kids. They were safe and sound in their beds. Liza was resting comfortably as well. As I walked down the stairs I began shaking my head at the thought of what I had accomplished. I looked up as if someone was looking down upon me and gave a great big smile.

I put on a coat and hat and took the phone outside to make some calls. First, to my sister, who had been a solid supporter, advisor, and who had been worried sick since I left. She cried when I told her where I was and what had transpired. She bombarded me with questions. "Are you sure they are safe at home with you? How did you get Liza to agree to do this? Can I talk to the kids or are they sleeping?"

I later learned that this new lightning round of questions would repeat itself many times over by those who were aware of my journey.

"They're fine but they're still sleeping. I can tell you a bit, C, and then I must hang up. I don't want to arouse any suspicion in Liza before I have to." Then I couldn't help myself. I whispered quietly into the phone, "We are safe in Milwaukee, big sister! Can you believe it?" We continued to talk for fifteen minutes and then said our good-byes.

Bruce was next and he, too, was surprised, yet happy, to hear what had gone down. Then, when I called Bobby, I almost lost the hearing in my left ear from his yelling and screaming. He was happy and, keeping in character, had to know every single detail.

Now awake, I made sure Liza was occupied in the house and then placed a call to my attorney. The enthusiasm in Julie's voice led me to believe that even she was surprised at the outcome. It also meant plenty of billable hours, as well as a huge challenge for her. After giving her a few details, she again asked, "Scott, you're telling me that the kids are with you in Milwaukee right now as we speak?"

"Yep. They are in bed sleeping from the long flight. I was too excited and slept for six hours. I'll rest again later."

After congratulating me, Julie was all business. "I want to make sure that tomorrow would still work for you with regard to Liza being served with divorce papers."

"That's perfect. I am going to be at work later in the morning and the kids are going to be at a friend's house so that Liza can get some sleep. The early afternoon seems like a perfect time to me. Let's proceed with the plan."

"Scott, things are going to get messy fast, and you should be prepared for anything Liza might try to do. Who has the kids' passports?"

"I do. They are safe in my pocket and will be with a friend within the hour. We wouldn't want her trying to sneak off again now, would we?"

I could not wait to get home the next day and see the look on her face. I imagined steam coming from her ears, like in the cartoons I watched as a child. Remembering that my marriage was about to end and the children's lives were going to be turned upside down, I took a few deep breaths and headed back inside.

My plan was a long time in the making and almost never developed. I knew well that things would get rough again quickly, but having the kids close to me made dealing with whatever would be thrown at me easier. I figured that it couldn't be worse than the hellish road I had just traveled.

The next day I went back to work. I saw a few of my accounts and brought my manager, Bob, up to date. He was happy but repeated his mantra to "watch my back."

I arrived home around 3:30 p.m. that fateful afternoon and met Liza waiting at the door with a paper in her right hand. Waving it in my face with spit flying, she screamed, "What the hell is this, Scott? What are you trying to pull here? Are you out of your mind? What is going on?" All appropriate questions for the person who had been just told that life as she knew it was over.

"Those are the divorce papers I filed, and I will also be requesting custody of Jonathan and Alexandra. Our marriage is over. Scott and Liza are over. You lied and deceived the wrong man, and you did an awful thing to our children."

Usually never short on words, Liza stood stunned and silent. This was my moment of Zen as I watched her boil with anger.

"You can't do this, Scott. This is not what we agreed to do when we were in Israel. Where are the kids' passports? I want them right now. Do you hear me?"

"You deceived me when you kidnapped our children. I trusted you and you trusted me. We both lied to each other, Liza. It's sad, but you and I are over. I suggest that we split everything down the middle, including our time with the children, which will be here in Milwaukee."

"That is never going to happen. You'll be sorry that you ever met me, Scott."

I walked upstairs to get away from her verbal assault.

Though I was not sure where things would lead the four of us, from that moment I knew in my heart and mind that I had done the right thing. No parent should ever do that to his or her children, and given the situation, no spouse should ever have to endure what I went through.

To say that things became tense in our home is an understatement. The cold-steel Israeli wall appeared, as I assumed it would. Ever focused on the children, I left to pick them up and allow Liza time to calm down. I suppose I should have stayed away a few more days, because she did not care that they were standing next to me when her next salvo of curse words and screaming commenced. I took the kids upstairs and explained that it was just a little disagreement.

"Please keep your voice down so that the kids won't have to hear you yelling."

To her credit, she hung in there for about thirty seconds and then stood within three inches of my face. Spit once again flew and veins bulged from her forehead, so I asked her to back away. She muttered something in Hebrew, English, Arabic, and a fourth unknown tongue under her breath, but I picked up most of it. She was red hot. I remained somewhat calm, hoping to keep myself intact as I watched her unravel.

I had to pinch myself so that I'd remember I was home with my children and not dreaming. She followed me from room to room, still yelling obscenities, while trying to make eye contact. My calm exterior and straight face only fueled her anger more.

Liza's tirade continued. "You will have to leave this house now because I can't live in it with you. I want you out now or I will call the police on you, you son of a bitch. I am leaving tomorrow with my children and you can't stop me. You think you're so smart. Well, we'll see about that!"

A fair statement for sure from the woman who was never, ever wrong. I understood that we should not sleep under the same roof, so I politely asked her to go to a friend's house to live.

You'd think by her next outburst that I had asked her to cut off an arm or a leg—or be without her children for four-and-a-half months. I did my best to remain calm. "I want to make this clear to you, Liza. Let me know if you don't understand something. I am not leaving this house. I am staying. If you don't like it, leave now."

My balance as a human being was returning, and my desire to be with our kids remained as strong as ever. I had a sharp attorney, and we had already set up plans and put them in motion, while Liza was left standing in a kitchen in Milwaukee with no lawyer, poor past decisions, no parents to help protect her, and a husband she had sorely underestimated.

Many things were back in my control, yet I regret to this day the damage one adult can do to their children by talking trash and lying. From that day on, Liza used every moment that she spent with the children to bolster her own ego while painting me as a horrible father and man.

Two trusted friends advised me not to bad-mouth Liza to the kids. "You will be tempted and every muscle in your body will be aching to, but you must resist for the sake of the children," they said. It made sense not to mess with little minds for one's own gain.

I spent more time at home keeping an eye on my children. Jonathan would ask me why Mom was so angry. I told him little, except that Mommy and Daddy were working through some issues. He knew what his mom was upset about because she told him every day. I proceeded to play, read, feed, and nurture the little ones, hoping to keep them balanced. Ally was less affected because Liza used Jonathan as her main sounding board.

Eventually, she retained an attorney named Larry. He proved to be cruel and vicious, as if he had a personal stake in the outcome greater than simply winning. I, on the other hand, had a lovely and talented pit bull representing my interests.

Neither of us moved out, instead choosing to 'tough it out' as long as possible. After one week, the idea of divorce and just how serious things were began to settle into Liza's head. A few days later, I came home after work to find Liza on the phone with her family. She handed me the phone. "It's my father."

I decided to hear what Joseph had to say. "Scotty, what is happening there? You told me when you were at my house that you would be coming back with Liza and Yoni and Alexandra. What are you doing, my son? I want you all here with me. This is not good, it is not good. They need to be here and I want it very much. You must come back now with Liza and the children."

One of her brothers, apparently feeling the same way as his father, took the phone. "Scotty, why are you doing this, man? You are not being honest here and they belong back home with us. You need to bring Liza and the children back home, my brother. Liza should be in Israel, man. You were not honest with us. Come back soon. Don't worry, everything will be okay."

I agreed with her brother regarding my honesty and asked if he would like to come over, as did I, to discuss it further. Not happy, he continued to tell me where my family belonged, and that I had broken a promise to them.

Having debated in college, I enjoyed the sparring and allowed him to speak without interruption. He did not afford the same courtesy to me, and I finally stopped him cold. "Look, man. Please take care of yourself and your family and I'll do the same with mine. Stay out of my business or you will find me on the phone with your wife on a daily basis discussing anything that comes to mind. You did share some very personal things with me, remember?"

Sensing he had little effect on me and remembering a few of things he had told me in confidence, he handed the phone over to his father to continue the interrogation. Liza was in the other room listening, but she did not dare walk into the room, likely hoping that they could move my emotional meter and sense of fair play toward their side.

Joseph began to speak again with his heavy accent. "Scotty my son, what are you doing with my grandchildren? You sat in my home and looked me in the eyes and said that you would bring my daughter back with the children." His tone was sharp and his message clear; he was not happy. However, he then told me that I was welcome back in his home and that I should continue to make arrangements to move.

I wasn't sure just how I wanted to approach this. On the one hand, he was our children's grandfather and father of my soon-to-be-ex-wife. On the other hand, he did nothing for my children or me and even aided Liza in her quest to do whatever the heck she thought she was doing.

I decided to be tough. "Joseph, this is my family we are discussing, not yours. Stick to your family's business and I will deal with mine. Also, I do not appreciate the fact that you allow your daughter to behave in such a manner. Is this how you raised her? Is this the kind of behavior you allowed in your home? Would you have allowed your wife to take your first two children and move back to Egypt without you? I'm their father, and you let me and your grandchildren down, sir!" I kept on and did not allow him to reply for two minutes.

"Scotty, you come here and we will make things good for you and your family," he persisted.

The time had come to end things before I stooped too low. "I am not coming back to Israel and if you want to see your grandchildren, you'll have to come here to visit them. I have nothing else to say to you. Would you like to speak to your daughter?"

I handed the phone to her and received a predictable scowl in return. *Well done,* I thought, *let him stay in Tiberius with all of his kids and grandkids and their stories about their grandfather's terrible behavior.*

As the days went on, Jonathan spent time in kindergarten while Ally stayed home. I made sure I got home in time to pick him up at school. My struggle every day became the delicate balance of calming the curious boy's mind and giving him support and love.

In the evenings, I'd give the kids baths and read to them. It allowed me a few hours to break down some of the confusion they were feeling. We laughed and talked until bedtime. "Daddy," Ally asked. "Why is Mom so mad at you? Do you want her to leave us?"

"No sweetie. Of course I don't. We just don't agree on where the four of us should live. Please don't worry. We'll work things out." I constantly reminded them that they were wonderful children and loved by both Mommy and Daddy.

Liza would usually stay in the kitchen on the phone with a glass of vodka, speaking to anyone who'd listen.

Four weeks had passed since we arrived back home. I was working and still living in the house with Liza. My manager continued to remind me to "watch my back," and I did. "Hey, don't eat any food she gives you and for heaven's sake, make sure that you sleep with one eye open." I was already feeling the pressure of divorce and its potential effect on my children, so worrying about being poisoned or stabbed in my sleep only made matters worse. I tried to focus on other, less painful topics.

Work was going surprisingly well, which helped us all. Liza had begun making noise with her lawyer. They were coming at me with false accusations that immediately put me on the defensive, as if I was the one who had caused this madness.

They wanted me out of the house and Julie and I said, "no way." I told Liza, "I will not leave this house. Tell your attorney this as well. When I get custody of our children—and I will get custody, Liza—it will be you who'll be leaving this home."

She screamed back, "That'll be the day. You will leave the home one way or another. Don't you..."

I stopped her in mid-sentence and said sternly, "If you make another threat to me in any way, or if I feel as if you are out to physically harm me, I will go to the police and have you arrested on the spot."

I had already moved into a separate bedroom to try to ease the tension. Unfortunately, the kids wondered why I changed rooms, and I was honest, because Liza had told them everything.

They seemed mostly happy, but I noticed them struggling in school. Jonathan was having more trouble than Ally, as Liza continued applying more pressure on him to take her side on all issues. I'd hear her telling him in Hebrew, "I need you and love you more than your father. He hits me and says awful things. You are my life, breath, and soul."

I knew that Liza was filling their heads with negativity and attempting to manipulate them in many ways, but I still had no answer to that. Julie asked Liza's attorney to have her stop this destructive behavior and he passed it on to her, but telling someone that they cannot talk to their kids was a line no judge wanted to cross. She didn't stop, and I too asked her to leave them out of this mess, which sadly seemed to only empower her.

In the fall of 1991, a guardian *ad litem*, Marty, was assigned to represent our kids' best interest. As an attorney, he had the opportunity to do this several times in the past. Julie made sure we had a copy of the 1988 Hague Treaty handbook on international child abduction handy. This would help guide us on proper international abduction procedures moving forward. We proceeded to go over these pages for hours and hours in Julie's office. I was beginning to understand the basic laws as they applied to international custody cases. Julie was able to grasp details fast and would often explain the ins and outs as she understood them. Sipping sodas and reviewing a table full of material, we'd try and make decisions based on law, not emotion, which, happily for me, proved to be easier for her. Eventually, Julie presented Marty with a summary of the Hague Treaty for International Child Abduction for his review.

I was happy to help in any way I could, as Marty was new to the Hague Treaty and its specific guidelines. We also had to provide him with a list of character witnesses, which proved to be both humbling and awkward. Once again my life would be an open book for anyone and everyone to view. I told my godson, Sean, "Giving the names and numbers of people who will say you are a good parent seemed to me like a setup. They are only going to say nice things because I provided the list. Does he ask questions that would actually trip someone up?"

"It's a good thing you and I are so close, or I'd have to sell my expert knowledge of you and the kids to the highest bidder!" Sean exclaimed.

"You're a funny young man. Nice payback for the guy who helped to raise you since you were four."

"Seriously, I think that you are a great father and have done a great job while Liza has done everything in her power to mess them up. I can't wait to get on the stand in court, under oath, and tell 'em what I've seen."

Sean was an honest kid, who, despite our close relationship, would be truthful about everything. The fact that he spent more time with the four of us than anyone else was a plus as Julie and I saw it.

My brother once told me that if you are wondering why many things occur, just follow the money. This was true in my instance, and plenty of people were being paid on Liza's and my behalf. Thankfully, both Carole and Bruce were able to lend me money during this tough period.

I was paying for three attorneys, who billed $150 an hour each. The financial stress was enormous. Liza proved to be a master of pleading poverty. Our monies were still combined and our savings plus my paycheck were being used to pay lawyer bills, keep our lights on and keep food in the house.

Keeping the very curious Jonathan and his younger sister from their parents' mess was a challenge. Two years older than Ally, Jonathan had an idea that things were not good, although I tried hard to shield him from any possible fallout. Mommy was still constantly using him as a sounding board, and Ally was now getting an earful as well. I became furious at Liza's behavior.

It was all I could do to try to be a positive role model while not overtly defending myself or trashing their mother. I often bit my lip when Liza verbally attacked me in front of them.

"Watch what you eat." "Sleep with one eye open." "Move out, you nut, and take the kids with you." "Do you want the number of someone who will scare the crap out of her?" "Hire a bodyguard." These were but a few of the many suggestions thrown my way by friends and family. I took heed but maintained that I would not leave the children, as I continued to take the high road while constantly remaining alert.

Medical releases had to be signed so Marty could talk to my therapist, John, and Liza's therapists, too. Arrangements were also made for psychological evaluations for the four of us. Another cost that we could not afford, but happily the children were in Milwaukee.

I learned during these months that there is no limit to how many times you can be dragged in to see a court commissioner or a judge. The fees kept adding up and I paid my half, which was tough. When I devised the plan to see to the safe return of our children, I did not factor in the tens of thousands of dollars that would be spent to secure their butts on American soil. Preoccupied on figuring out how I was going to pull off this crazy scheme and bring them home had been my only focus. Having no prior legal experience, I assumed ten grand would cover everything. I was young, foolish and way off on that estimate.

During a September 23, 1991 appearance in front of Commissioner Grady, I was ordered to pay all expenses for the family. Liza, still unemployed by choice, had no intention of finding work. I was asked to provide all of our financial records. I had hoped for a different decision, which would have provided me with temporary placement and made her come up with some cash as well. To my surprise, this didn't happen. Commissioner Grady awarded us joint legal care and custody along with joint physical placement.

The initial trial date was set for July 20, 1992 but was pushed back to October 1 due to other trials. This meant living in the same house together for at least eleven more months. Having to wait to hear the judge's decision began to play havoc on my nerves. No one had control, and both sides were posturing to keep the other from making any more progress.

In November 1991, we had to call the psychologist to set up appointments for the four of us to have individual psychological evaluations. This cost was $1,400 and did not include his testifying in court with his findings. I had to tread very carefully during this process, as professionals who literally had my future in their hands were testing me. Follow-through was never one of Liza's strong suits, so I set up the appointments.

We were closing in on three months since our return from Israel, and the tension in the house continued to build. We called our attorneys and complained, which settled things down. Each of us were posturing and pushing our agenda on the other and anyone who would listen. Little things would always become magnified because we were living under the same roof. Occasionally, we tried bringing it down a few notches. Both Liza and I stood our ground, because giving up a centimeter was a sign of weakness and neither of us wanted to appear soft to the other.

The law can be a funny thing. I figured that this was open-and-shut case with her losing custody of the kids. It turns out that even if you kidjack your children and have your butt flown back to the States, you can still be free to interfere with the kids' daily lives and ignore rulings by the court.

Liza's no-filter approach with regard to talking was about to backfire. "I will be moving to Israel with my children, and no one will stop me, you'll see," she said to the commissioner, smiling.

No one could stop her from showcasing this destructive behavior, and she proudly stated to our friends and anyone who'd listen, "This makes me happy to say that I'm moving to Israel with Yoni and Ally. Why should I stop when they are my kids? I can tell them everything, and I do. Scott has to pay all of our expenses and I'm not looking for work because it's too difficult for me right now."

I maintained my steadfast position that this behavior was not healthy and that it in fact harmed our children. However, it continued, and she was confident that the court would give the kids to their mother, not their father; everyone knows this, she figured.

Our children asked me if I was moving to Israel as the future of their residency became cloudy to them. Julie and I complained to Marty and he did speak with Liza, but little changed. He, too, had limits as to what he could do, and Liza was not intimidated by him. I, on the other hand, maintained a healthy dose of respect, realizing how much influence, if not power, he had over the final outcome.

Liza's lawyer tried tripping me up at every turn with motion after motion and counter motions as well. He asked Julie if he could observe me in our home with the kids. We declined. Julie called me one morning. "We're not about to allow them to evaluate you without permission and I am not about to give it to them, Scott. Just keep doing what you're doing. You are doing fine and I believe they know that. They're nervous and are grasping at straws. They want to see if we will bend or break and just what we are made of. Stay strong and don't let them irritate you."

"So when do we unleash the pit bull and kick their asses? I am sick of being attacked when I did nothing wrong. I don't want to appear weak. Shouldn't we be going after them and backing them into a corner?"

"Don't worry. I am confident that when we get to court and I lay out all that has occurred, the judge will see things our way."

"Does this mean that we'll win?" I asked hopefully.

"I cannot make any predictions, Scott, but we have a fair judge and a good case. As for the pit bull, we are doing everything we should at this point. Yelling and being overly aggressive is not what is called for right now. I understand that you are under enormous pressure and want this to end soon with Liza's head on a platter. You will notice a change in me when we enter the courtroom and I will do everything I can to make sure the court sees our side. Until then, we just need to stay on top of things and you need to spend as much time with the children as you can, so that Liza's attorney doesn't accuse you of not being there for them, as I suspect he will."

By now, all of the correspondence from Julie—and there was plenty—was going to Bobby's store so that Liza would not be privy to our strategy.

1991 was coming to a close and we were still nearly a year away from our October 1992 trial date.

Things moved slowly and every day was a challenge. I was helping raise two young kids, holding down a job, and battling Liza and her attorney, all the while living under the same roof. Not all days were tense because it simply took too much out of us. At my suggestion, we held family nights where we pretended to be united for the children's sake. We even laughed a bit to ease the tension, but I calculated every move, as this was a battle to the end, and the time for friendship and understanding had long since passed.

We continued supporting three attorneys as 1992 came in with a bang. Everyone was asking for money and it was all coming from the same dwindling account. Marty asked Liza and I to fill out questionnaires. It was standard procedure in a custody case to have us answer these specific questions, as it would bring clarity to where Liza and I stood regarding many important child-rearing issues.

The questions included were: Is there anything that you can give the children that the other parent cannot? Are there any areas of concern you have regarding the other parent's ability to care for the children? What have you told the children about the divorce?

The list consisted of thirteen questions with a personal follow-up interview. We also had to once again provide all financial information, which I hated doing because I regarded it as private. I found Marty to be smug, but he did seem to see us both pretty clearly. His role was a difficult one, but Liza provided a rare transparency few others could match. I hoped that this would shed light on who and what she was all about.

Our attorneys asked us to vacate our home on alternating weekends to ease the tension. The living situation and arrangements were convoluted and one parent in the home at a time was looked on as best for everyone. I declined, as did Liza.

One evening after Liza had had some drinks, she approached me in our kitchen while the children were asleep upstairs. She was so close that I could smell the vodka on her breath. "Okay Scott, I can't take this crap anymore. You're not a man. You're a coward and a liar. The kids hate you, I hate you and everyone knows you're wrong. Give me the kids now, you baby. Be a man and do the right thing."

She called me more names, continued to insult my manhood and pushed me hard, but left no bruises. I almost lost it. My rage and desire to get her to stop were almost too powerful to control. Knowing that one swing from me would lay her out flat, I forced myself to walk away. She must have planned on "taking one for the cause" because her badgering, pushing and face-to-face confrontation did not stop for ten minutes.

Continued attempts by our attorneys to change our housing arrangements did not work because Liza and I would not budge. I remained focused on my children. I had their friends come over for play dates, took them to parks to play and made sure they had plenty of time with Dad.

"Dad, Mom said you're taking her to court. Is that true? Why would you do that? She did nothing wrong."

"Well Jonathan, I want you and Ally to know that your mom is right. We are going to court. We have to take care of some adult things and the court will help us. Please, please don't worry about this. I'll let you know what happens when were done."

Ally sat on the living room floor listening. She was less affected as her mother continued to confide in her older brother more often.

Liza spent a lot of time on the phone while I worked. She called Israel often and rates in 1992 were still costly. She was charging things and taking money for whatever she wanted, and the attorneys were trying to intervene in this matter because cash was tight and they rightfully wanted to get paid.

I visited my friends when things became too much. One couple was Shelly and Patty, Sean's parents. We talked and share ideas while laughing about the past. They thanked me for playing such a big role in their son's life. I told them it was an honor.

Sean and I are very close to this day and I treasure the relationship. Ever since he was little, Sean loved to play with soldiers and G.I. Joes. His excitement for all things military eventually grew into an enlistment in the U.S. Navy after high school.

He served in the first Gulf War. Thing is, if he felt that Liza was the better parent he would tell me and anyone else who asked. Thankfully, he did not, but he wasn't coming back from overseas until March of 1992.

I needed my now not-so-young godson Sean to fill out some information for Marty and return it to him. I also wanted him to testify on my behalf in court later in the year, but I presumed that he would be back at sea somewhere in the Mideast. Later, I notified Marty of a two-week leave Sean had obtained and an appointment was made for them to get together.

In February 1992, things were inching forward toward the trial and a final decision. Our psychological testing was both grueling and complete, and I had prepared well for it. Although it was difficult, I managed to get through it without any glaring mistakes, though the pressure to show that one is not a moron was in the forefront of my mind.

Our psychologist, who would be giving the evaluations, had published a book that discussed testing, results, how to perform the test and even possible questions. I thought it a good investment so I purchased one and studied it for three weeks. The information was helpful before test time. I was happy he was published and doubted Liza knew about the doctor's book.

One snowy morning a month after testing, I received a call from Julie. "I wanted to let you know that I have received the report from the psychologist and it is very much in your favor. As a matter of fact, he appears to see Liza in her true light. You can't hide much with all the questions and interviews you four took part in."

Thrilled at the great news, I asked, "Does this mean that we can count on the good doctor's support in court?"

We went over his findings and conclusions twice until it sank in, and after twenty-five minutes Julie finally had me convinced that this was a crucial victory for us. "Judges tend to lean heavily on the opinion of the children's attorney and the findings and recommendations of the psychologist. Liza's attorney also has this report and will not be pleased with the findings. I suspect he'll try to file a hearing to have it tossed out."

"Even better, Julie. I want them on the defensive for a change. Thanks so much for this great news. I've been so worried, but now her side can sweat a bit."

Liza's attorney did just what Julie predicted and launched an offensive the next day, once again filing a motion strongly objecting to the findings in the psychologist's report. His objections were filled with many inaccuracies, but we still had to go in front of the judge to discuss their concerns. I could hear the cash meter ringing as the three counselors arrived once again at Larry's request.

I was mentally tapped out and the stress of appearing in court again was taking a toll on me. Larry knew all too well that these findings would be used in court under oath when the good doctor was testifying. Both sides knew that the judge would hold much weight in these findings, as well as the recommendation of Marty, the children's attorney, when giving his final decision.

In what was yet another expensive and emotional day in court, we were told that the psychologist's findings would be admissible. Listening carefully, I looked down at my shoes, shook my head and let out a gigantic sigh of relief. I knew what this meant to our case. The good news helped me stay focused and regain my strength, while continuing to motivate me in my quest to permanently be with my children.

Liza continued to tell anyone and everyone that she was going to Israel with the children. She even called Julie and informed her of her plans. Everyone involved knew her intentions. Then Liza received a huge break.

Much to my surprise, Israel decided to sign The Hague Treaty making extradition of minors easier. As I had already read up on this, I knew that she still had a large hole to climb through. If she was ever able to return to Israel with the children and decided again to keep them there, I would have to go through massive legal maneuvers to get them back to the States. Even then, it could take a lot of time and even more money with no absolute guarantees. A big concern for sure, but we had a trial to prepare for and first needed a favorable decision.

My 401(k) took a heavy hit as we began dividing up our assets. We were only four months away from the big day. It hurt, but I still had the two best kids sleeping in the room next to me every night. Surprisingly, we did a fair job of dividing things up and split the pie into two, as the law required.

Liza complained to Larry, who in turn filed another motion that stated I pushed her around and that I smoked pot. She also claimed that I was never home with the children. She lied on all points except one. I never touched her. I was usually home watching her, as well as our children. In fact, I was home during the evenings more than she was.

Unfortunately, one day she found a small bag of marijuana in my desk drawer and informed me that she had called her attorney. Things were already quite tense since I was being hauled into court every thirty to forty days. I was worried about the missing bag because it was mine and it had my fingerprints on it. Though it was a small amount and I used it sparingly, who knew what lengths she and her attorney would go to use this against me. I did not want to find out so I searched the house from top to bottom. No bag. I looked again and again and still nothing. I walked outside to think when it hit me. It had gone missing only that day, and Liza had not left the house. Could it be there? Sometimes dumb luck is the best luck of all. It was in her purse and I found it! I took it, left the house and got rid of it for good. I had dodged yet another bullet that most likely would have caused major damage.

The warm, beautiful, and difficult summer was ending and we both managed to stay alive and in the game. The leaves were turning colors and I could smell autumn in the air. Liza filed another injunction claiming all sorts of things that were not true. Lies and more lies had to be proven false by my team in court, which continued to frustrate Julie and me.

Cornered like a true Wisconsin badger, Liza and her attorney threw anything they could my way. They were good at always putting me on the defensive and making my side prove any new allegations to be false. Julie, always ready for them, was beginning to show some anger as well because they would not let up.

It was now September 1992. Cooler days were here and I could feel my uneasiness growing as the trial moved closer. The October court date was holding firm, and I was once again weak from staying on guard and fighting every second of every day.

Yet another attempt was made by Larry to throw out the psychologist's findings, with further accusations hurled in my direction. This time I was accused of coming home late and often intoxicated. I had to find more time, more money, more stamina, and more patience to keep myself together, as their continued attempts to change the direction of the case were taking a toll on me.

I pulled up to the courthouse for the latest motion against me wondering if the lies told about someone usually equaled a similar action on the part of the court, or no action at all. Could this hurt them in the judge's eyes?

The judge once again sat before us and listened to all three attorneys closely. It was emotional and tiring, with Julie using precision in her delivery and flying the psychologist's flag for all to see.

After the testimony was concluded, we were told to come back in two hours for her decision. I had developed a case of the "Tic-Tacs" and walked around with those one-and-a-half calorie mints in my hand as if they were prayer beads. I ate them like candy and had extremely fresh breath to boot. I became accustomed to the sound of my shoes as I'd walk up and down the corridors waiting to hear my fate.

I still could not believe all that had transpired in the eleven months since the four of us landed in Chicago. I never expected this to play out so long after what Liza had done. I figured any judge would be appalled at her behavior and that I would get the kids.

I was wrong, and shocked at how long the child custody process took.

Her Honor came in and we rose. After being seated, I noticed Julie fidgeting with her rubber band on her wrist. I knew it calmed her down and asked her if she had an extra one. She smiled and said that she did not, so I offered her a Tic-Tac, which she almost always declined. This time she took one. *What does that mean?* I wondered as she popped it in her mouth.

It probably meant that she wanted a Tic-Tac, that's all.

The judge looked up from her bench and said, "I am going to deny the injunction. That's it. I don't feel that there are reasonable grounds here. You will proceed to trial in three weeks. Thank you."

Another victory for the good guys.

The big battle grew closer and both sides were posturing and making last minute preparations with their witnesses. It was hard living with the enemy and we were both exhausted. Liza was still telling the children many negative things and I remained powerless in the face of her destructive behavior. Jonathan was angry and confused and my heart went out to him. We talked, and I constantly told him how wonderful I thought he was doing. "Dad, I don't know why mom is so upset," he confided. "Do you really want to take us away from her? She needs us and we have to take care of her."

This from the lips of a five year old, but I had some gentle answers. "Sweetheart, Mommy and Daddy are not doing well. We are not going to stay together, but we will always love you and Ally very much. We are all healthy and have a nice home so everything will be okay. Please focus on your friends and school. This is what I want you to do. Do you think that you can do this for me, big guy?"

Concern filled his little eyes. "I'll try, Daddy, but Mom is really mad." His concern for his mother, yet none for his dad, led me to believe that her mind games were continuing to have a negative effect on him.

I decided that I needed one more person to appear in court on my behalf. Another lesson I learned was that it is really hard to get in contact with someone who is on the *Dwight D.*

Eisenhower aircraft carrier heading to the waters of the Middle East. You don't pick up the phone and call, and letters take a while to catch up with a battleship two football fields long, although I knew of no other way.

Sean was at sea. In order to contact him, I first had to go through the Red Cross. This was the single point of contact for all those wanting to quickly get in touch with military personnel at sea. A few days later I received a call from Sean. "What's up, Godfather?"

"Well, I need your help and it's a big one."

I updated him as to where we were in the final weeks before the trial and what I needed from him. He replied, "Let me see what I can do and I'll be in contact with you."

"How are you going to be able to do that? You're on a Navy carrier somewhere. You can't just pick up a phone, can you? By the way, where are you exactly?"

"Can't tell you that because it's classified, but I have friends on board who will help me out. Also, remember the Red Cross is now involved, so it should not be a problem."

"Thanks, my boy. I love ya and I'll wait to hear from you. Please be safe."

"Aye aye. I love you, too. Please send my love to the kids as well. You'll be hearing from me."

Sean had no problem taking time off and returning home to see friends and family. He managed to get permission from all of his superiors and was on a jet back to Milwaukee within two weeks. Thing is, he'd just had a ten-day leave the month before. I don't know how he managed to do this, but he said he was dying to help the kids and me in this most serious of matters.

◆◆◆

CHAPTER 16

THE FIGHT ESCALATES

◆ ◆ ◆

I WAS A nervous wreck on October 1, 1992, our fated court trial date. Bobby asked me if I wanted a ride to court. Thanking him, I declined, wanting time to think and psych myself up.

Tic-Tacs in hand, I made my way to the family court floor and found Julie sitting on a bench, rubber band on wrist, and focused on some papers in her lap. We walked to a private room to discuss the procedures of the day one more time. Julie wanted to know how I was doing. I lied and said, "Fine." I didn't want her to be shaking like me.

My exterior exuded a fairly calm and collected professional flooring representative, but inside I felt knotted up, wishing I had some control over my future. I ran earlier that morning and did some deep breathing, which helped calm me down to the level of only mildly freaking out.

Julie appeared fine as we waited for the judge to arrive in court. I asked her if she was ready to kick some ass for the children and myself. "Yes, I am," she said with a confident tone and a slight smile.

"You've done this before and I haven't. Got any last words to help calm me down?"

"You'll do fine in court. We've gone over things many times and are well prepared. Let's go in and take our seats."

As we entered the courtroom, calmness washed over me. Liza and her attorney were already there as we made our way to the large table. Liza smiled and nodded to me; I flashed a hint of a smile back. Each of us showed confidence and a readiness for battle.

Marty sat to the left of Julie and me. He had a boatload of papers. We exchanged greetings and I had the urge to ask him which way he was leaning. I didn't, thank heavens, as Judge Gary Gerlach, the man holding all the power in his hands, entered the room. The judge's black robe commanded respect as he seated himself above the court.

After opening statements, Liza's attorney immediately went on the attack. He had a lot to overcome and much to prove to the judge, including Liza's kidjacking of our two children. Also, the report from the psychologist whose findings were less than favorable for his client sat on the judge's desk.

Julie followed. I appreciated how she appeared to be calm and succinct as she stated our case. I was happy to have her handling my case, and like her, I too remained focused and highly determined.

The court reporter would earn her keep as the nonstop words were plentiful. In all, the trial would last nine painfully long days. The judge asked Marty to stand. He explained to the judge who he was representing, and what he would offer the court during the proceedings. Each attorney had been here before; all were professional and articulate.

The psychologist was the first witness on the stand. He, too, had testified many times before. The three attorneys had many questions for him, and Liza's attorney tried to dispute his findings and testing methods.

Marty also asked numerous questions, making sure that he and the judge understood the doctor's findings and how he had reached them.

Julie carefully led the doctor through his multi-paged findings on the four of us. She focused a lot of attention on his findings regarding Liza.

Concerns for the children (not present during the trial) were at the forefront of his mind when testing and interviewing us. I listened closely to every word, looking for encouraging signs for our side. He had greater concerns for Jonathan than for Ally, perhaps because he was older and had received the brunt of Liza's anger and manipulation.

The psychologist testified that Liza continued telling Jonathan way too much and treated him like her sounding board rather than a five-year-old child. I knew this all too well, yet I felt that I had let the little guy down by not protecting him more. Did he think I could have stopped her as well? Thankfully, he did not.

Julie and Marty made sure to cover all of the psychologist's conclusions and recommendations, but Larry once again picked only the ones he wanted on the record, mentioning little in the way of his client.

In the end, the doctor stated that according to his testing and interviews, his opinion was that the placement of the children should be with the father.

Pleased beyond words, I looked over to my right to catch a glimpse of the kids' mom. She whispered to Larry and did not look my way. The psychologist went on to state that I appeared a bit arrogant during the interview. He was correct. I was confident, frightened, and exhibited a whole slew of other emotions during that process. I hated being mentally poked and prodded.

My scores on the testing phase were better than Liza's, which usually pointed to the parent who would receive the primary physical placement.

The kicker, which now confirmed what I had thought for some time, was the psychologist's description of Liza: "A narcissistic personality coupled with sociopathic tendencies. This is a woman with deep-seated psychological issues."

He stated that while he had some concerns about me, his findings regarding Liza far outweighed any of those concerns. The issue of Liza taking the children to Israel and not returning with them to the States weighed heavily in his report. He worried that if she were given primary physical placement, she would do everything in her power to limit my access to them. He further stated that if she were given custody, she would be on the next plane to Israel, effectively knocking me out of the picture completely. He suggested counseling for the children to help straighten out the mess of divorce and the brainwashing tactics Liza had employed.

I turned toward Julie to make sure she liked what the doctor had said. She looked quite pleased, but said that we had a ways to go. We adjourned for the day.

The next morning other people testified including a psychologist named Hava that Liza had seen. It became clear to Julie and me that she was biased, and her testimony carried little weight. Also, Hava had neither tested nor interviewed me.

On day three our neighbor, Ann, testified on Liza's behalf. She called Liza a good mother who always had the best interests of the children in mind. She wasn't so kind to me. Ann, in court and under oath, claimed that Sean and I had "frolicked around naked in our backyard on several occasions all year." She lied. My godson Sean is fifteen years younger than I, and we have known each other since he was four. I played a big part in his upbringing and am like a big brother as well as a father and close friend to him. It is true that he was at our house often and had a decent relationship with Liza. Furious that she would make such an accusation with my children's future hanging in the balance, I dug my fingernails into the palms of my hands.

What a sight we must have been! Milwaukee winters are not made for any type of outdoor naked frolicking!

I figured she had very poor eyesight or was lying under oath to help Liza gain custody. Needless to say, the relationship with my neighbor ended after that day.

Each afternoon concluded when Judge Gerlach felt it was time for us all to regroup, as emotions ran high and our minds were fried.

As incredible as it seems, every evening after talking things over with our respective lawyers, Liza and I headed back to the same house in separate cars. I could see that she felt the stress of the last few days, and I was fine with that. We each still had to testify and I was as ready as ever to go toe-to-toe with her guy. One evening, after six days in court, she asked me if I wanted to stop this silliness and forget about what happened. "What is it that you want?" I asked her.

"Just let me take the kids and you can come to visit anytime you want," she offered. Knowing she was dead serious, I didn't bite and replied something to the effect that we were going to see this through to the end.

Our young ones heard nothing from me about the last few days, but once again Mommy needed comfort from the two who had not yet celebrated their fourth and sixth birthdays. Powerless to stop her yet wanting to silence her, I attempted to deflect her pleas of help to our kids when I could.

As the trial continued, I had a few more people testify on my behalf. Sean traveled the farthest and helped the most. When asked about the different parenting skills he observed, Sean fairly pointed out Liza's love for the children. He also disputed any negative comments that were made about me. He did chuckle when asked to respond about the alleged naked frolicking incident while categorically denying everything Ann had said. He called me "a wonderful father and role model who is always there for the children." He also said that I put their interests first and stated that he could not, in all honesty, say the same about their mother.

Two days remained. It was my turn to be grilled by the three lawyers. Larry went first and attacked me from the get-go. He questioned my religious knowledge and desires. Next, he questioned my dedication to my children and stated that I was a poor parent. I wanted to yell back at him because he had been coming after me for over a year, but I knew that we were close to the end and would not give him that victory. I sat up on the stand for an hour-and-a-half answering questions while getting nods of reassurance from Julie, which I needed.

"Scott, did you not go to Israel under false pretenses and lie to get Liza to agree to come back with you? Didn't you promise her that you would move back there if she agreed to help you sell the house and pack up your belongings?"

"Yes I did."

He tried to cut me off, but I was not going to stop until I fully answered the question to my satisfaction. The judge asked me to continue.

"Larry, I was not finished with my answer. Liza kidnapped our children and took them under false pretenses to the Mideast, for heaven's sake. I suffered, as did our children from her behavior. I would not be here today in this court if I had not figured out a way to get our children home. I broke no laws and our children are safe right here in Milwaukee, where they've been raised. I would do it again if I had to. Your client messed up big time, and I came to the rescue of two little kids who would otherwise be without their father."

This was my first time being on the stand, and I was both nervous and well prepared. I was usually short with my answers, trying to add comments only when I thought it would help. This time, though, I would not answer in short sentences.

"How could you try and take the kids from their mother, Scott? Isn't that the very thing you are here for?"

"No. I'm here *for* my children. I plan on being a big part of their lives. Liza kidnapped Jonathan and Alexandra and wanted to keep me from them. I did not."

"Will you agree that you were out of control when you lied to Liza? She came back to the U.S. under false pretenses. They're her children too."

"I'm going to presume that you have children, Larry. Would you allow you wife to kidnap them and keep them from you?"

"I'm asking the questions, Scott. I asked you..."

"I maintained complete control, Larry. That's why I'm here today in court. Had I not kept my composure my children would be going to school in Israel. Instead, thankfully, they're going to school right here in Milwaukee."

"Liza has stated in depositions that you hit her and pushed her. Is that true?"

'No."

"You are telling me in this courtroom under oath that you never hit Liza."

"Yes."

I answered all of his questions while continuing to focus my sightline on Julie. She would reassure me after answers and didn't intimidate me.

In the end, Larry received little, if anything, he could use against me and I could sense his frustration as he walked back to his client. This seemed oddly personal to him.

Marty, the attorney and guardian *ad litem* who was appointed to represent our children, was next and I answered questions ranging from what I would do if I received primary placement to the type of parenting skills I thought I had that were better suited to raising the kids. He inquired about my job, the hours I worked and our house as well as if to paint a picture of the environment in which the kids might be raised. "How about Liza as a mother?"

I had to walk a fine line here because Julie had warned me that trashing Liza too much would not look good to Judge Gerlach. Yet, how could I not call her out big time and show how very much she had hurt our children and me? How could I not tell the court what a despicable person I thought she was?

How could I hold back emotions of hatred that flowed powerfully through every inch of my body?

The answer, of course, was the children themselves. I owed it to them and their future to stay strong. Once again my well-oiled fifth gear kicked in and was running smoothly as I did my best to answer the many questions.

He finished by asking me if I believed I would have the best tools to raise the children. A trick question, because he had covered this earlier. Now sweating, I once again explained why I thought I was best suited to raise Jonathan and Alexandra, throwing a few arrows at Liza in the process. "Honestly, a parent who withholds children from the other parent, and does so in a far-off country while showing no remorse, is best suited to play a supporting role, at most, in the rearing of children. I am not a professional, but I am closer to this case than anyone, and am surprised that she was not jailed for this behavior. The cost in time and money, along with the intense stress, makes me think that she should have to answer for this horrible behavior."

I was fairly calm while stating this and glanced at Julie to make sure I hadn't gone too far. She smiled and nodded ever so gently to show her approval.

Marty had no further questions for me. Now it was Julie's turn.

We flowed through questions that were designed to show the court what I had gone through since Day One as well as every possible detail pointing to me as the better parent. The psychologist's findings came up several times. I made sure I did not smile and gloat on the stand. In the end, I testified for four hours with no break. There were no further questions and I was dismissed. Weary, I made my way to Julie and said quietly, "I need to pee."

We broke for lunch, and Julie and I dined in the café downstairs. We discussed the morning's testimony over sandwiches, chips and sodas. She was pleased and said I did very well on the stand, which meant a lot. We each made some calls after lunch, since the trial would not resume for another hour.

It was now Liza's turn on the stand. I could tell she was shaken. She tried to remain calm, which was surely out of character, as Julie meticulously grilled her. She asked her to explain to the court why she decided to keep the children in Israel and cut off contact between them and their father. Liza explained that she had had "enough of the U.S." and wanted to be back at her home. "I was not happy here and did not know what to do. What can I do? I am their mother and they belong with me." Momentarily flashing a smile, she added, "I did what any mother would do. Scott lied to me when he came to Israel. I didn't want to come back."

Everyone in the courtroom could see that the hole she was digging was getting larger and deeper. Liza's long answers to direct questions gave the courtroom a transparent view into the workings of her mind. She maintained all along that she did nothing wrong. "My children belong with me. I'm their mother. No one will take them from me. This court can't keep me from them."

I glanced over at Marty and her lawyer Larry to see their expressions. Both looked stoic. I turned back to watch Julie in action as she carefully continued to show the judge why Liza was ill suited to raise our children. In the end, Julie, the pit bull, did a great job.

Liza trashed me, said I smoked pot, and also said that I was not a good role model for the children. Her opinion carried little weight as experts and others saw things differently. I just stared directly into her eyes with disbelief.

Marty cleared up any gray areas that the court may have had and treated Liza with what I thought were kid gloves, which surprised me. Throughout the last year-and-a-half, I noticed that commissioners and judges showed Liza more sympathy and understanding than I ever expected. She played the "poor me" card as well as I had ever seen. I felt that I was always the one being portrayed as the "bad guy" and Liza was the misunderstood woman who needed the support and sympathy of everyone.

In the end, Marty asked every question he needed to give the judge a clear picture of what had occurred and why it happened. Her attorney finished up with an attempt to show a Jewish woman from Israel whose heart was in the right place but whose actions might have been a bit unorthodox. He tried hard to show her as the wronged mother who needed to be with her children for her very survival.

I was truly surprised, yet grateful, that I had not been accused of abusing the children. Liza had told so many lies under oath that I assumed she would play that card and play it hard. It never happened and although there would have been no proof, accusations could have dragged the case on, or even worse.

After Liza's testimony, Marty cleared up a few final financial pieces of information regarding the division of property with Judge Gerlach. We were finished. All sides rested.

I wanted the decision at that moment almost as badly as I wanted to be with and raise my little ones. Completely worn out, I could not bear to wait another minute. No such luck, as we were told that court was adjourned for the day and would resume at ten o'clock the following morning.

As strange as it sounds, Liza and I took the kids out for dinner that evening and "acted" like a family. This was to be our last meal together before the divorce. I had suggested we do so, as the battle was over and the casualties were going to be tallied up in the morning.

I didn't sleep well that night. I thought about scary slasher movies and wanted to be alive for the verdict in the morning. I knew Liza was desperate.

I spent the night quietly on the floor of the kids' room. I wanted to be close to them that evening for all sorts of reasons. I wondered how they would handle whatever decision we received in the morning. I was so weak and drained from my marriage and all of the subsequent fighting. I felt even worse for two young children who had no business being wrapped up in their parents' mess.

◆ ◆ ◆

CHAPTER 17
DECISION DAY

◆◆◆

THE NEXT MORNING arrived, and I was alive and tired. The kids slept safely in their beds. Outside, a sunny day smiled and waited for me. We roused the kids and had a friend come over to watch them. I didn't wear a tie and jacket that day. Never comfortable wearing one, I figured that the decision had already been made.

I hopped into my Mercury Sable, Tic-Tacs in pocket, and Liza got into her Renault Alliance as we headed to the same location. To say I was nervous would be an understatement. There were no guarantees to the outcome, though I did ask Julie on several occasions to make a prediction.

I had done what I had set out to do and never gave up. I learned much about others and even more about myself along the way. I always tried to keep moving forward, either mentally plotting or actually executing my plan. I stood my ground and said, "No way. This is wrong and I will not allow this to happen to me or my children, no matter what!" Although many times people or circumstances tried to stop or slow me down, I remained focused on my final goal.

Lastly, I listened to my gut. Sure the mind is in charge, but being in tune with and acknowledging my gut instinct allowed me to have a heightened awareness of situations. This primal sense often steered me in the right direction.

Dressed in a gray pant suit, Julie appeared well-rested and relaxed as we met in the hallway outside the courtroom. We stepped into a side chamber to compose ourselves and talk about future possibilities. She had the experience and I had the children to think of, so together we came up with plans, depending on Judge Gerlach's decisions.

I spoke first. "Julie, I want to thank you for believing in me and my case. I also want to thank you on behalf of my children, whom you have met. One day they will be grown, and I will play the major role in their upbringing. Regardless of the outcome, they will know that a woman named Julie cared enough and believed in what I was fighting for to help the three of us so much. Also, thanks for keeping me in one piece. Knowing that I had you firmly on my side to guide me in my quest to be with my children gave me strength that I desperately needed."

She smiled, momentarily looking down at her papers, and then her eyes met mine. "Scott, I hope the judge awards the children to you. He should; we showed him exactly why it is the right thing to do. Honestly, I'm not sure that I would have been able to keep it together if I were in your shoes. You have been down a long and difficult road, and I am impressed with all that you have done. I have learned some things myself and thank you as well. Let's head into court and take our seats."

My heart raced fast and my hands began to sweat as we walked into court for the final time. Bobby, Bob and Howie, my three closest friends, were seated in the back of the courtroom. We hugged as they wished me good luck.

We reached our table and sat down. Liza, Larry, and Marty were also seated and ready to begin.

"All rise," the bailiff said as the judge entered the courtroom.

After greeting us, Judge Gerlach went on to say that this was one of his most difficult and complex cases. "I have made decisions on the Findings of Fact, Conclusions of Law, and Judgment of Divorce." I sat forward in my chair, riveted to his every word.

The judge continued, stating that the psychologist's report pointed out repeatedly that Liza would do everything in her power to obstruct contact between the children and their father if she received primary placement. He found the psychologist's findings to be more credible then Dr. Hava's, because she did not test Liza or me.

He pointed out that she had intended to keep them in Israel and that I brought her back under false assumptions. He went on to say that the children were closely connected to both parents. The report found me to be somewhat guarded and defensive, stating I had some "unresolved feelings of anger and loss over my relationship with Liza."

Regarding Liza, the psychologist found her to have "a history of poor judgment, immaturity, rebelliousness, irresponsibility, hypersensitivity to rejection and criticism and a strong need for approval."

Listening to these findings I asked myself, *How did I pick this person? What attracted me to someone so damaged?*

Judge Gerlach continued reading: "These people tend to have poor work records, poor marital histories, and are likely to blame others for their problems, accepting little responsibility for themselves." He finished by saying that the test indicated "a deep-seated psychopathology associated with antisocial personality patterns, passive-aggressive personality disorder and difficulty in establishing relationships."

He continued talking and my mind wandered.

Wow! I finally understood Liza now that a professional pointed out what made her tick. I felt bad for her, but not when it came to Jonathan and Alexandra. No one on the planet was allowed to mess with them, including their mother.

I had made a promise with myself to fight and push hard to have the opportunity to be a big part of their lives. Not an issue a year and a half earlier, Liza would change all that.

Once again I thought about the day in Athens, looking at the world map in the travel agent's office. I shook my head. *Who could have known that a single decision to hop a flight to Tel Aviv would carry so much weight?*

The judge paused, looking down at his papers. He then said, "Scott Lesnick is awarded primary physical placement of both children nine days every two weeks."

I looked at Julie and said, "This is good, right?"

My very supportive friends stood up yelling, "Yes!" several times. The judge didn't threaten to clear the courtroom for this outburst, and I smiled when I heard them.

It was over, and I had accomplished what I set out to do. I'd be able to stay connected to my children's lives, and that was all that I have wanted since they were born.

Liza began to cry. The judge continued. He ordered me

to pay Liza child support in the amount of $1,250 a month. He also ruled that she could take the children to Israel for the summer each year. Outraged, I expressed my feelings to Julie. After all Liza did and tried to do, it seemed like she was getting off easy and receiving far too much. I could not go along with her leaving again, even if papers were filed in both countries.

In addition, he awarded the house to me and half its equity to Liza.

I spent a few moments with Julie and my friends, collected my thoughts and headed home.

The next few days were difficult as Liza moved her things out. She begged me over and over not to allow us to end things this way. She wanted to take the kids with her, but I asked her to leave and call me on the phone. My job would be to protect my children against a woman who would do extraordinary things to get what she wanted, with no thought of others.

Things could have ended that day in court as Judge Gerlach read his decisions. I would have worked with Liza and bent the placement guidelines if she had treated the children well and no longer attacked me. She chose instead to do neither.

I understood her better than ever thanks to the doctor's report and knew how to deal with her issues—or so I thought. It isn't easy to stop someone from talking, and my damaged ex-wife had a ton of things to tell our little ones.

I had the difficult job of explaining to two young kids that their parents were not going to be together anymore. Sure, Liza had filled their heads with lies. Yes, she had built me up to be a monster. Of course, they were upset and confused. I did my best to ease their pain and loss.

The courts did not seem to care or perhaps had little power in stopping her from building herself up in the kids' minds to deity status while busting me down to scum status. Highly manipulative with the kids, I was powerless to stop her.

She continued breaking our kids' spirits. Liza's psychological makeup led her to believe that she always did right by them. She also desperately needed them to believe that she was as great as *she* believed.

I remained focused on our children. I could handle her. I could deal with whatever she threw my way.

Well, almost anything.

◆◆◆

CHAPTER 18

A NEW BEGINNING
FOR THE FAMILY

◆◆◆

I BEGAN THE task of single parenting with pleasure and ended most nights by lying on the couch alone and zoning out. It proved to be difficult, and I needed to get into super-single-dad shape, which would take some time. Now 1993, I had survived four months of raising Jonathan and Ally alone. My parenting skills were improving with every passing week. Our house became a regular hangout for their friends. Jonathan said that we had "cool snacks," which was, of course, by design.

Liza now lived in an apartment in a place where she did not want to be and saw the kids less than she ever imagined. I waited for her next move, knowing she had too much time on her hands and didn't approve of the court's decision, or her ex-husband.

I continued to grow my business and income. Liza began preparing to take the children to Israel for the summer. The court felt that with all of the proper papers in accordance with The Hague Treaty filed in both countries, the kids would be protected.

I worried constantly when she took them that summer and knew that her family would have a thing or two to say upon her arrival. Not one of them came to the States to help her and show support during the year-plus that we were in and out of court. Even during the trial they were absent.

Though I could to talk to the kids while they were in Israel, I did notice a distance in their voices. Their mother quickly broke down all of the positive work I had done to help keep them balanced. Counseling had helped, but she reprogrammed them constantly.

They were gone for two months. I got to the airport three hours before their flight arrived. It must have been difficult for Liza to step back on a plane to the States, but to her credit, she did. I waited as they exited baggage and passport control and received two big hugs. I was relieved and so very happy to be holding them.

The year ended with minor breakdowns in placement, with Liza changing the schedule as she desired, creating much tension, which she probably wanted. She also went to their school and pulled them out of class to spend time with them. Teachers and principals voiced concern, but Liza remained vigilant in her quest to be with them whenever she wanted.

I sensed a stronger and reinvigorated woman after she returned from Israel. I filed a motion because she flew out of control with regard to following the court orders of placement. She acted like the law and rules did not apply to her.

My routine at home with the children continued to be a challenge, and Liza wanted more action even if it hurt her in the process. She proved this by having Larry file a counter-motion. In it, they accused me of not being religious enough. Liza wasn't religious either except when under oath! They suggested I bad-mouthed her.

She also wanted me to have a shorter amount of placement with higher quality with the kids. When I'd take Jonathan to Cub Scouts, Liza would show up. Brownies with Ally went the same way. Now upset that I was taking them to family counseling without letting her know, she complained to her attorney. I did let her know on many occasions and asked her to join, but she declined.

She wanted primary placement, more money, and lawyer fees paid by yours truly. No fifth gear needed here, just a lot more money, time, and self control so that I wouldn't do something stupid.

With so many lies, too much time and energy was spent that I needed for the kids, though I hadn't lost focus on them, I moved between work, kids, and lawyers. Too bad that the same judicial system that awarded this father primary placement of his kids, when it was not yet in vogue, had little ability to halt Liza's destructive and wasteful behavior.

I needed more adult interaction, as most of my time continued to center around the children. I had little time and even less energy. I did manage to meet a wonderful lady named Jane. She and I hit it off and spent some time together, but not much with the children. I didn't want them to get confused. Jane reminded me that women could be kind, intelligent, gentle, honest, and giving. I had lost this feeling over time as Liza's attempts to change the placement arrangements failed on several attempts.

I had always contended that the court's reasons regarding our specific arrangements did not matter. As long as I spent most days with the kids, I could offer balance and honesty in their lives. But I did feel that it did an injustice to the kids, allowing them to have so much time with their mother. I would gladly have welcomed a civil and kind divorce that allowed both parents to share equally in the rearing of the children, but the other extreme occurred. Although never much of a fighter, a fighter I became and discovered that I could hit back very hard if necessary.

I had been doing the single-parent thing for about 22 months and was doing better than the kids, who were now four and six years old. Their mom continued to mentally abuse them and tried to change custody, to no avail. School was a challenge for Yoni, but Ally was doing pretty well.

I would attend all of their school functions alone. It felt weird to do so, but they always knew that they could look up and find their dad. One morning, Yoni came to me and said, "Dad, I want to go live with Mom."

"Why do you want to do that, sweetie?"

"Because she needs her son and I love her."

"I know that you love her and that's good, but we are going to keep things the way they are."

The thing is, I never told the little ones anything until the divorce was final. Their mom told them everything and added lie after lie to get their sympathy. My inability to stop her from messing with their minds and souls continued to worry me. There were no laws to stop her from talking, and the judge did not want to give her less time with them than she already had.

Thankfully, my personal life was about to change. The kids' lives were about to become enriched in ways they never imagined.

◆◆◆

CHAPTER 19

MEG

◆ ◆ ◆

THE YEAR 1994 did not offer much in online dating services, so if you wanted to meet someone in your city you perused the personal ads in the local newspaper. I responded to a few "women seeking men" ads with little success.

Lonely, I longed for some adult conversation, as much of my time was spent with a five and seven year old. One night after reading several books to the kids while lying on the floor between their rooms, I decided to glance at the newspaper. The biggest news that day for me appeared in the personals, and I happily found it.

Meg Marredeth was looking for a man and having little success. This would be her last week of trying this particular method, because things did not pan out as she had hoped. I liked her snappy, funny, and honest description and decided to call. By the way, does everyone say they like to go on long walks? Anyway, I received a call back from Meg and we made plans to meet for lunch.

Long brown hair and a beautiful face were the first things I noticed. Slender, with a great smile, I liked what I saw. We greeted each other and sat outside.

It was a sunny July day and I asked if she would mind if I kept my Ray Bans on. She said "No problem," which is a positive sign to me. We ate and laughed, and she was cool with my light-sensitive eyes. "I love to travel, but I have not been to many places yet," she told me.

"I, too, love to travel and have seen a few places."

We spoke about her job as an advertising sales rep. She liked it, but marketing was her passion. The more we talked, the more I got glimpses of a balanced and happy person.

I wasn't ready to tell her everything because, frankly, I did not want to frighten her away. "Would you mind paying for lunch because I only have a hundred?" Always joking, I thought I'd test her early.

Not missing a beat, she got me back, "Wow. I only have a hundred dollar bill as well, we'd better use yours!"

"How did you know I was joking?"

She smiled. "I could just tell." We finished lunch, I paid, we talked more, and parted ways after an hour-and-a-half. I knew that I wanted to see her again and hoped that she felt the same way. I cut out all the usual guy crap and called her later that day to thank her for the great lunch.

She called me that night and we talked for an hour. She simply felt right, honest, and more natural than any woman I ever knew. To say we clicked is an understatement, and we never looked back!

Our third date would be the Scotty-tells-all-date. I took the chance early, and out of respect decided to tell her about my two kids. I didn't want us to get too emotionally involved only to have her back away later.

To my amazement and joy, Meg was intrigued, but not shaken. She really liked me, liked our connection, and was willing to see how things went. "I thought you were going to tell me that you were dying or moving to China or something," she said calmly.

"Nope, I'm not going anywhere. You did hear me when I said I have custody of two little kids? One sweet girl and one adventurous boy."

"I heard you. Do you have any pictures?"

I pulled out two photos and she thought they were adorable. I explained that the boy was a handful and the girl only half a handful. She smiled and gave me a kiss.

I had children to protect and felt us growing closer by the day, as did she, and so began our long and semi-private courtship. After two months, we both knew we were in love and committed to the relationship. There would be no kid involvement at this point, to protect their fragile souls. I remained determined to keep them out of our relationship until we decided we were going to marry.

I learned early that Meg was special. Intelligent and funny, she had the maturity and wisdom of someone much older than her twenty-seven years. Perhaps having two sisters twelve and fourteen years her senior played a part. I am seven years older than Meg but am always trying to catch up to her. I could tell that she was one strong, sharp woman as I slowly began to bring her into our lives. My children were my top priority, so it took a year of dating before they met her. Both kids took an instant liking to her. We went to Chuck E. Cheese's or played in the park. We had dinners at home and the kids continued to enjoy spending time with her. "Is Meg going to live with us?" Ally asked one night.

"No, my love, not right now. We're just good friends. I want her to get to know all of us better. Is that OK with you?"

It was, and Jonathan liked the idea too. He loved to challenge Meg with questions, and she'd smile back and answer each one with honesty and humor in a calm manner.

A week later at 9 p.m., my phone rang. "Hello, Scott, how are you doing?"

I could sense that Liza had something on her mind.

"I want to cut this crap. I want the kids back, you know they want to be with me, and I need them. You don't love them like I do. You took them from me and you should feel terrible!"

"Liza, I will only say this once so listen closely. If I felt that our children would be free from your messing with their minds and that I would never have to go through what I just went through, I'd talk with you. Thing is, I don't trust you and, sadly, never will again. You blew it, and you know it. You lied, you manipulated people, and bent the truth horribly to suit you. The fact that they are with me more is what is truly best for them. If you were a normal parent who actually put the best interests of our children before yourself, as I try to do, things would be different. I'm going now. Bye."

Tempted to change the number, I relented because the kids needed to know their phone number too, so hiding it from their mom would not work. Sure, I was free, but not completely.

I didn't want to waste time or money by hanging out with attorneys again. Liza continued to complain that I was not a good parent. I had to play defense again against more lies and false innuendo. Since the trial, I'd had little rest. She continued creating new baseless charges in an attempt to gain full custody of our children. I had no choice but to go to her attorney's office with Julie to get grilled by a man I detested.

I felt surprisingly confident in his conference room as he tried to show that I, not Liza, was taking advantage of the custody arrangement among other things.

"Scott, did you not keep the children from Liza on three separate occasions that they were supposed to be with her?"

"Nope."

"Remember Scott, you must be honest and that everything you say is being recorded. We will be back in front of the judge. Are you saying inflammatory statements to the children with regard to their mother?"

"Nope."

"Scott, I sense some hostility toward me and your answers are without much depth. I'd like some more explanation to my questions. Can you do that?"

"I have answered your questions to my satisfaction. If you are looking for something more from me, then keep asking questions. Heck, here is a slice for you to chew on, Larry. Your client lies to you. She has lied under oath in court. She will lie to anyone anytime to get what she wants. This is fair play in her world, and I believe that you know and support this obstructive behavior, which in turn only hurts my children, sir. As for inflammatory statements, Liza is the only one doing this. I have asked her to stop because it hurts our children. I wonder why she never brings up the children and the effect her poor judgment and behavior has on them."

I had a lot of pent-up aggression toward him and had little opportunity to hit back. Looking stunned while squinting, he just stared back at me, shaking his head. Julie asked me to stay on topic, which I thought I was doing. It must have been my A.D.D.

He grilled me for two hours and I mostly answered with one or two words after my little speech. I had said everything during the trial, and he was sadly mistaken if he thought I'd give him anything new to use against me.

Julie had her turn with Liza and much of the same clueless, yet highly confident lady appeared.

"Liza, Scott has reported that you are keeping the children on days they are supposed to be with him. Is this true and, if so, why?"

"Scott is the one messing with the schedule and keeping me from my children."

"On June 20th of this year, just one-and-a-half weeks ago, did you keep the children an extra day?"

"I made a mistake or two with the schedule. I am sorry. Is that all?"

"Liza. I have information here that shows more than six times you broke from the court-ordered schedule. Would you like to see this?"

"Yes."

Julie reviewed people, places, and times to show everyone that indeed Liza continually strayed from the court-ordered schedule.

The damage to the kids hurt, but not knowing whose house they were going to be at was just plain mean. Still, no attorney and no judge could force Liza to stop talking to the kids in negative ways, so she continued to be herself. Not so surprisingly, she never denied the other times she took them out of class or kept them from me. Did either attorney get much that day? I suppose we gained more information and we all got to know each other a little better, too.

The following week the attorneys held a status conference in front of the judge. In this setting, the attorneys meet alone in the judge's chambers to discuss any new events that could change the court's original decision. They decided to leave things as they were with a warning that lost time with the kids to either party departs from the original ruling and would not be tolerated. Even if I wanted to give Liza more time, my hands were now tied. Her attorney had brought up the topic of continuing the child support as the two years the judge had granted her would soon be coming to an end. Another court hearing would be needed.

I called Meg to let her know the outcome. "I still have the kids and need to be a good boy."

"Good. Let's celebrate this weekend when they go to their mom's. I want to talk to them before that, though, and make sure they are doing all right."

"She's now coming after me for more maintenance. Babe, I'm tired of fighting, constantly being on the defensive, and worrying about the kids. Oh, yeah, and I still owe $20,000 to two attorneys. Why am I constantly being attacked? She created this awful mess and is looking to be rewarded for her poor judgment."

"You need to remember how much the kids need their father. Without you, they are stuck with a mother who can't help them and continues to actually hurt them. You are a wonderful man and a terrific father. I want you to know that. You need to stay strong and fight for them."

Self- doubt still crept into my mind at times. Happily, Meg continued to keep me focused, balanced and mostly positive. Fortunate to have her in my life, Jonathan and Ally had grown quite close to her as well.

Because my brother and sister were older than me, they had collected their entire share of our mother's inheritance. I only had two thirds, so I asked them to help me pay some bills and keep afloat. Paying $1,250 a month to the person with no job who messed things up to begin with seemed highly unfair to me.

We had to see another court commissioner before the judge would see us, as Liza and her attorney wanted an extension on maintenance. In October of 1994, they argued that, "Liza has made significant progress in being able to accept the divorce and the rearrangement with the children. She believes that Scott has increased his earnings and that he is in far superior financial condition."

A true statement. I was working and doing well. She did a few massages a week. This could have ended, but Liza never expected things to turn out as they did so she pushed all the time to see what more she might get. How she paid her lawyer bills after pleading poverty so often is anyone's guess.

Judge Gerlach made it simple when the day to see him arrived. The attorneys gave their spiel. After some thought, he came back with the following ruling. He ordered me to pay six more months at $1,250 per month. After such time, mainte- nance would be terminated. This meant I would be free of all financial obligations to her in 180 days. Although not thrilled, I could live with that decision. To help out, Bruce and Carole each lent me $5,000 to help pay lawyer bills. I paid them back within one year.

I wish that things had improved in 1995 for the children and me, but the opposite was true. Liza and I fought. She would still go to the children's school while they were in class and spend time with them. This didn't help matters, and little was done to stop her except a stern warning by the judge. We were fierce enemies. Still on the defense, Julie and I continued to disprove all accusations hurled my way in front of court commissioners or judges.

Meg and I were doing well, and she continued spending more quality time with the children. They loved having her around. I began to have her spend even more time with the three of us, because we were sure that we would get married.

Although things were progressing well at home, the little ones were still confused. "Dad," Jonathan asked, "why are you and Mom fighting so much? She says that you are trying to take us away even more and that she does not know what to do."

What could I do to help him? Almost everything Liza told them was fabricated.

"Sweetheart, I want you and Ally to see your mother. The judge made this decision, not your mother or me. What your mother said is not true and I cannot say anything more because this is adult stuff. I want you to focus on school and friends, please."

This occurred often, and I knew that holding back information would be the best way to protect them. It made me look awful in their eyes, though, because Liza would badmouth most people associated with me, leaving the children to figure out who they could trust. Remarkably, Meg was somehow insulated from Liza's verbal attacks because she knew the kids were getting close to her. As I look back on this period in my life, Meg, the kids, and my job helped me maintain balance and focus while being attacked for three straight years.

1996 was a good year for me. I made inroads with the children and showed them that they were fine with their father as the major adult role model and caretaker. They struggled, but again Meg would help keep their lives balanced. She was not living at the house, but we were gradually becoming a foursome. We picnicked at parks and were regulars at the zoo and museum. Movies were a big deal and the four of us tried to go to one every month. Homework became easier for us all with Meg taking the lead.

"Do you think I'm doing well with the children?" Meg asked me one day.

"Babe, you are a wonderful female role model and are doing great. I see how the kids are comfortable around you and how they ask you any and all questions they can think of."

Never having children of her own, Meg learned to be a mother while dealing with young ones who had gone through some very difficult times.

The kids and I moved forward to 1997, and once again the year was filled with failed yet expensive attempts by Liza to change the status quo. In and out of court, yet nothing changed. Jonathan and Ally were now eight and ten and developing their own opinions with regard to the mess that Liza and I had created. They were still attached to their mom and were being manipulated by her at every turn. Meg continued to be a pillar of strength and wisdom they often went to for guidance.

In 1997, Meg and I had been together for three years when

I asked her to marry me. She said yes with a huge smile, and we started to make plans for a June wedding. The kids would be nine and eleven and they had developed a strong bond with her. "I want to be a flower girl," Ally said to me one day.

"Why can't you give me away, too?"

"I can do that too, if you want, Dad."

"Hey Dad, is there going to be a limo at your wedding?" the not-so-shy Jonathan asked.

"I think so. You'd better confirm that with Meg."

Like she had done almost from the beginning, Meg took the role of stepmother-in--training and ran with it. Realizing she was taking on a lot of responsibility, she maintained a certain calm and confidence that emanated outward. People, including the kids, simply felt comfortable around her. I knew I got lucky in many ways when I replied to her ad in the newspaper. She claims that she was very fortunate as well. I reminded myself that Meg is usually correct!

Less time spent in front of judges and court commissioners allowed the four of us to live our lives in peace. The courts had spoken and Liza tried, lied, and lost every time. No changes were made to the original rulings. It was over, or so I hoped. She owed me money for insurance and other items that she chose never to pay, totaling many thousands of dollars. I never challenged her on it, deciding instead to continuing move forward with my life.

◆ ◆ ◆

Meg and I were married on June 7, 1998, by a beautiful lake nearly four years after meeting. We had a wonderful time with our family and friends and danced until midnight. My sister Carole agreed to watch the kids while Meg and I snuck off to our honeymoon room.

The children spent time with their mother while Meg and I went on our honeymoon. No courts, no kids, and no battles worked out well for Meg and me. We enjoyed ourselves immensely and had time to relax, reflect, and plan more for our future as a family as well.

A few weeks after arriving home, our phone rang. "Dad, it's Mom and she wants to talk to you," Jonathan yelled from upstairs. I reluctantly took the phone from Ally and walked outside. I had nothing to say to her and little patience for her crap. "Hi Scott. I wanted to tell you that I am moving back to Israel next month."

I immediately began doing a dance of joy inside my soul as I listened to her reasons for making this big decision. "I cannot take it anymore. I am tired and want to be home. You win. Please take care of the children. I know Meg will do a good job in my place."

I smelled something brewing, but I could not put my finger on it. What in the hell was she up to now?

She spoke for ten more minutes. I held the receiver away from me ear to avoid hearing too much of her "poor me" speech.

She was leaving, which would be great for Meg and me, but not so good for the kids. Her main reasons for leaving were her need to be home, never finding work in a good economy, and no more money from me.

I wanted to say so long forever, yet I knew what to do, so I dug down deep inside to try and locate a sympathetic nerve ending. "Liza, why would you move away from your children?

This will crush them. It does them little good. You must be strong for them, stay here and be a positive part of their lives."

I had put the children's interests ahead of mine once again and almost hated myself for doing so. For Meg and me, life without Liza around would be easier. No more court, no taking the kids from school, and more balance for the four of us. "Scott, my mind is made up. We need to talk to the kids and explain to them what is going to happen."

Then it hit me. The psychologist's findings regarding Liza, coupled with the fact that she would no longer be receiving money from me, painted a clear picture of a narcissistic individual who also had no cash.

I ran inside to the den where Meg was reading. "Babe, I've got something to tell you. Liza just told me that she is moving back to Israel next month."

"You've got to be kidding me! Tell me you're serious?"

"I'm serious, love. She is moving home with her parents." She sat silent with her mouth open for about five seconds. We hugged and literally danced as we celebrated the awesome news. After a few moments of sheer joy and shock, we turned our attention to Jonathan and Alexandra. Could they handle this? Would they be able to cope with the huge changes in their lives?

Several beautiful parks surround Whitefish Bay, so we had our choice that day as we packed some food and the kids into the car. Meg provided support for all, and I would tell the kids the news.

To say neither one of them was happy with the news was an understatement. They cried and wanted to talk to their mom at once, so we packed up and headed to her apartment. They cried, pleaded, and cried some more, but Liza had made up her mind to go home to her mom and dad. What kind of mother would do such a thing? I wondered.

Cries of "Please Mom, don't go" were heard, and our hearts melted for them. I knew all too well the type of person we were dealing with now.

My visit to Eilat seemed so long ago as I looked at their mother with disdain and at our children with such love. The next three weeks were great for Meg and me, both personally and professionally. The children didn't have it quite as easy. They spent more time with their mother, and Julie made sure that all the legal papers were filed in both countries, according to the Hague Treaty, to protect the kids. I had my guard up and Julie, although momentarily shocked at the news, made sure Liza's attorney cooperated as well. "Daddy, will you please drive Mom to the airport in Chicago so we can all be together?" Ally asked.

"Of course, my love. Is it okay if Meg comes, too?"

Both kids probably realized that this would be especially good for the ride home and quickly said yes.

The five of us drove down to O'Hare International Airport and said good-bye to Liza. My battles with her were over. The ride home was tearful, mostly quiet. I once again thought back to the day I stood in the Athens travel agent's office looking at the huge world map fifteen years ago. So much had happened since then.

The kids were nine and eleven and Meg and I were working hard to stabilize them. With their mom back home in Israel, we were able to work on their minds and souls with little interference. They became healthier, and we were able to get them to agree to go to counseling as well. It wasn't easy for any of us, but Jonathan had it the worst. Bright and inquisitive, he was troubled by many of the things his mother had told him over the years. "Dad, Mom said you hit and shoved her. Is that true?"

"No, Johno, it is *not* true."

"But why would she say that if it wasn't true?"

How to answer? I wanted to say, *Your mother is a child who deeply wanted to be with you and your sister and lied, cheated and hurt whoever got in the way of accomplishing this objective. What she failed to realize in her limited capacity is that she only hurt you and Ally by lies. You got confused and hurt, too.*

What I said was, "Johno, when you are older, you will understand better. Please know that while Meg and I will not tell you everything you want to know right now, we will if you want us to one day. Meg and I are strong and our relationship is very good and I promise we will help protect you. We will never lie to you and will always do what is best for you and Ally. That is our promise to you, my love."

Meg and I thought that getting a dog would be a nice addition for the family. We hoped it would help the kids heal better too. The kids loved the idea. The four of us drove to Hilbert, Wisconsin, to a working family farm that also breeds Golden Doodles. There we met and picked out an adorable pup we later named Jazz. He turned out to be better than we'd imagined and we all fell madly in love with him. Jazz was intelligent, friendly, and helped the four of us to relax.

The courts granted Liza permission to see the kids over the summer. I vehemently opposed what Julie and I perceived to be a huge mistake, but it had no effect upon the ruling. I told Julie that this would not turn out well. She agreed that things could get ugly, but the Hague Treaty papers were now signed by Israel, and U.S. courts gave permission to Liza to fly them over there.

Liza began making plans to "bring them home," as she put it, in June of 1999, for two months. Attorneys were still going back and forth to make sure all the papers were filed in Israel and translated so that the Hague Statutes were followed. Milwaukee would be the jurisdiction where all final decisions would be made.

I argued, unsuccessfully, that Liza could not be trusted and that laws meant nothing to her. I called Julie and asked, "What is to prevent her from keeping the kids again after all that has happened? Who would make her return them?"

Julie assured me, "Nothing will happen until the proper papers are filed. We have to abide by the court's ruling whether we agree with it or not."

"I understand all of that, but if she keeps them there, what in the hell are we going to do? Better yet, Julie, what am *I* going to do?"

"All we can do is to make sure we have covered all of the bases and filed all the documents needed to protect you, Meg, and the children."

I knew that Julie had all of the legal papers put in place, yet I still had an empty feeling in the pit of my stomach. I had the law on my side, but the law moves slowly.

The court ordered Liza to pay for someone to fly with the children both ways due to their ages and the length of the flight. Once again, Liza ignored the order. The flight was only one day away, so I had few options. Upset, I had grown to learn that the person claiming to be their mother, and who had now abandoned them as well, was not good at the one job she so cherished. Unfortunately, if I didn't allow the kids to see their mother, it would have put them in an awful position. Once again, I had to decide what would be in their best interests, almost keeping them in Milwaukee.

However, since Liza did not hire an adult to accompany Ally and Yoni to Israel during the summer of 1999 as ordered by the court, Meg and I talked to the airline officials to ensure that the crew watched over them. As promised, the flight attendants kept a close eye on our two unaccompanied minors. They arrived safely in Israel and called to let me know.

Meg and I now had two months to get to know each other without the responsibility of the kids. Of course, we worried and talked to them often. They were back with their family in Israel and, sadly, our deprogramming and gentle love approach was quickly broken down.

Soon, I'd discover another reason why Liza left her children behind in America.

◆ ◆ ◆

CHAPTER 20

ISRAEL, AGAIN

◆ ◆ ◆

TWO WEEKS BEFORE Jonathan and Ally were due to come home, Liza called and informed me that they were enrolled in school for the fall in Israel, "The children have filed a motion to stop you from bringing them back to the U.S., Scott."

Keenly aware that Liza was behind this latest attempt to live with our children in Israel, I listened as she lied to me yet again.

"It is the kids' decision to do this, not mine," she insisted. "What do you want me to do, Scott? They miss me and I miss them. They don't like it there any more than I did. Let's see how they do and we can talk, okay?"

"No, Liza, it is not okay. If the children are not on a plane back to the States in two weeks, I will call the police in Tiberius and contact the courts in both countries as well."

"Okay, do what you want, Scott. They are seeing a therapist here, they don't want to leave, and I am not sending them. I have to go now. Do you want to talk to them?"

Both Yoni and Ally expressed their desire to be with their mom. I knew all too well that this move would do much more harm than good.

"You've got to be shitting me, babe," were Meg's exact words when I called her at work to tell her the terrible news.

Although obviously upset, she quickly realized that we had a new problem that required our immediate attention. The foundation of our young marriage and the well-being of the kids would be stretched to its breaking point.

Wasting no time, Meg began researching attorneys in Israel. She found her fifth gear quickly and used intelligence, adrenaline, and anger to lead her to a lawyer by the name of David, who lived with his wife and kids in Tel Aviv.

I called Julie and said, "I told you so. Now what do I do?" After I explained the situation, Julie filed papers again in the States asking for the immediate return of the two minor children in accordance with the Hague Treaty. We also had to file in Israel all papers translated into Hebrew. The money meter was running full-speed again.

David, originally from New York, seemed kind and helpful over the phone. While not entirely straightforward with his information, I sensed that with the money we were sending him he'd quickly became a strong advocate for the safe return of the kids. Having two small children himself gave him a better sense of what we were up against.

David and I spoke every day or two. It didn't take long for me to realize that I would most likely be making another trip to Israel. He felt that it was imperative for me to be there once any formal proceedings began. My taste for the country continued diminishing as I associated anything Israeli with Liza.

David asked for $5,000 up front for his services. "David, I've never met you, and I am in a bad situation here. Money is tight, and I can't afford to have you steal from me. What assurances can you give me, besides our conversations, that will ease my mind with regards to being swindled?"

"Well, Scott, you have my word. You have my phone numbers as well as my office address. I can supply you with some references as well, if you'd like. Please understand that I, too, have a reputation here and it is a good one. I will fight hard for you and get all the help I need to get your children back to you and Meg as quickly as the law allows."

"That's all you've got, man?" I said jokingly. In my mind and gut, I knew that David could be trusted. I sent the money the next day.

Now I had to deal with my work situation. My current manager at work was Jeff after Bob had moved on. Jeff and I had a good relationship. When I apprised him of my situation he calmly said, "Well, are you going to go get them?"

I explained that I would be leaving soon and had no idea how long it would take. "You understand that it could be a while, Jeff, maybe even a few weeks."

Thankfully, he was understanding and told me to keep in touch with updates when I could.

Concerned on several fronts, I'd try once again to retrieve two innocent kids thrown into an international nightmare. Meg and I were married less than a year and I would be leaving her in Milwaukee for an indeterminate amount of time.

Meg had just started a new job and also had a kind and supportive manager. We were both lucky from a job perspective and knew it.

Saying goodbye to Meg proved to be extremely difficult. The fact that we did not know when we'd see each other again made it even harder. This was more than just another business trip; this was the business of life. Holding her hands in mine as I waited in line to check in, I whispered, "I don't know what to say to you, my love. I don't want to leave you, and I don't want to go there. I'm so angry at Liza for what she is doing. Also, I'm concerned for the kids. She's done quite the number on them again."

Meg looked at me sadly and said, "I understand, sweetie, but if you don't go and try to bring them home, they could be in real trouble. Besides, we'd be miserable without them here knowing what harm she has already done."

We hugged for a long time outside security, not wanting to let go of each other. With tears running down her cheeks, I blew her one more kiss before heading to my plane.

The date read August 30, 1999 as I walked by the departure board. I thought how wonderful it would feel to be heading out on vacation to one of the exotic locations listed. People were talking, playing games, or reading while waiting for their flight to board. As I waited for my plane, I became very angry. The kids had been doing well before they left, and now I was headed back for who-knows-what with people who probably didn't care much for me. Scared and determined, I hung my head low, staring at my sandals, and waited for my flight to board.

I had warned the courts, the judges, and Julie that this would happen and was repeatedly told that measures were put into place preventing Liza from keeping our children in Israel. I never bought into that argument, citing Liza's blatant disregard for the law on any continent. I muttered to myself, "What about school? My kids should be at home in class today." They began boarding the thirteen-hour flight. I got on and took my aisle seat, determined to correct this awful mess once again. I had absolutely no idea what waited for me once I landed.

I vowed to myself to hold back nothing as I headed to Liza's home turf in order to bring my children home to Milwaukee as quickly as I could. Trying to reason things out in my mind, I concluded I'd have to channel my anger into energy so I could see to our children's safe and speedy return. Israel would once again be the backdrop for a fight I did not choose. Once more, Liza would do everything in her power to prevent me from seeing, talking and leaving with Jonathan and Alexandra.

◆ ◆ ◆

CHAPTER 21

DAVID, SHMUEL, AND ANOTHER BATTLE

◆◆◆

A SMOOTH AND uneventful flight made things easier as I once again, regrettably, found myself at the Ben Gurion International Airport in Tel Aviv, Israel. I was nervous walking through passport control. I did not know if Liza's brothers had set up some kind of check to notify them of my presence. Adding additional pressure, I remembered that the last time I left this country was under unusual circumstances and passport control had a few issues with me. "What brings you to Israel?" the nice lady asked as she stared at my picture.

"I am here on business," I replied, not wanting to get specific.

"And how long will you be staying here?"

I didn't think of that one so I said with a smile, "A few months. I love it here."

"Where will you be staying in Israel?"

I plan on making Tel Aviv my home for a while."

"Have a good time." She handed me my passport.

I picked up my rental car, a four- door Citroen, and headed into the city to find my hotel. After checking in, I washed up. Not the nicest room, but I later realized that I could see the sunrise, as well as the beautiful Mediterranean Sea from my window.

I had an hour before seeing David, so I unpacked and milled about the city before my meeting with him at a cafe. I felt as though I was working undercover. I walked by the café a few times to see if a man I had never met before sat waiting for me, wearing some kind of hat and dark glasses. I decided to take a seat and wait as I ordered a coffee. People walked by and some glanced my way, but none were David. Twenty minutes past our scheduled meeting time my attorney and savior at large, David, walked up.

Dressed casually in pants and sandals with a button-down short-sleeve shirt, he spoke with a heavy East Coast accent. About my height, he was stockier with brown hair. We shook hands and introduced ourselves. We proceed to order some food.

"How was your flight, Scott?"

I yawned. "You know, long. I did sleep for a few hours though. I've got to say, it's really good to see you, David. I have a lot going on in my mind and I am hoping that you can help me fix this mess. I am worried sick and very concerned for my children. What great legal maneuvers have you come up with?"

"Look," he said excitedly, "I have already filed the papers in Tiberius and asked the court to have the children returned to you while the proceedings are going on. I believe they'll agree because it is in accordance with the Hague Treaty. I'm also getting help from another attorney named Shmuel. He has some experience with The Hague and is very sharp. One more thing Scott, Liza already filed a motion and the Israeli court in Tiberius gave her temporary custody."

My mouth wide open, I began to speak when he chimed in.

"I know this is wrong and we will fix it quickly, I promise. We have a court date of September ninth. They pushed other cases back and moved yours to the top as this is Hague related."

"Thank you David. I want to get together with Shmuel as soon as possible. When can you set up a meeting?"

"I'll arrange it for the day after tomorrow to let you get some rest. I have spoken to Julie in Milwaukee. Nice lady. She told me that Marty is going to be reassigned to the case in the States. She's not pleased with Liza's actions and is determined to see that this never happens again."

"Julie is wonderful. We warned everyone that this would happen. No regard for the law and a lot of hatred toward me makes Liza dangerous as well as expensive. I have a court date of October 19 in Milwaukee to put the hammer down once and for all. I need to be back by then with the children. Please do all that you can to make this nightmare go away."

I inhaled my food as David sipped coffee. Sensing my jetlag, he picked up the check and pointed me in the direction of my hotel.

The minute I rested my head on my pillow early that evening, I fell asleep. After nine hours, I awoke to the familiar sounds and smells of an early Tel Aviv morning.

David called on my rented cell phone to tell me that the State Department had contacted him requesting to speak with me. They needed clarification as to the attorneys I'd be using. More evidence of the power of the Hague Treaty in international courts began playing out before my eyes.

A quick three-way call to the U.S. State Department cleared up any questions. They were kind and even sympathetic to my plight, although they didn't offer to send someone to help me bring my children home the next day.

The kids were now enrolled in school in Tiberius. I spoke to them later that day. They seemed fine but were distant and had no idea that their dad was only an hour-and-a-half away. I could sense uneasiness in their voices, which I concluded meant that they were confused, as well as uncertain, as to what was going on.

Ally's Hebrew continued to improve. We spoke briefly and, closing my eyes, I sucked in every word as if it were oxygen.

The following day I drove to Jerusalem to try and relax, but mostly worried. As I neared the Jaffa Gate, I actually found a parking spot. Knowing that parking is usually difficult here, I figured this to be a positive sign of things to come. Slowly, I walked through the old city to reduce my anxiety level.

The September sun was warm, with temperatures in the 80s, and no clouds above. I made my way into the ancient market and, as always, people milled about selling anything and everything. Western tee shirts with all the familiar logos were plentiful. I liked all of the Middle East rugs and lamps. The different foods and their smells once again gave me reason to smile, as I sampled my way through the crooked alleyways. Languages seemed to be mixed between Arabic, Hebrew, English, French, and German. This place felt so primitive, as if I were back in the days of Jesus, simply taking a stroll.

I walked to the Jewish Quarter. I grabbed a table at a small restaurant overlooking the Western Wall and the Dome of the Rock with its beautiful golden top. A man played "Strangers in the Night" as I gazed off in the distance. I sipped my Coke through a straw and ate my second falafel sandwich slowly, as I pondered what would lie ahead for me in the Israeli courts. Did they speak any English?

A trumpet nearby now played a medley of songs. I dined by myself at every meal. I didn't have the usual desire to strike up a conversation because my mind and heart were elsewhere. Meg and I continued to speak every day. She was sick with worry for the kids and me.

The next day I put on my running clothes. I ran early in the mornings along the Mediterranean, which helped, but I had little else to be excited about. My path took me north toward Jaffa, and no matter how early I awoke, there would always be Russian immigrants on the beach exercising and swimming. They were moving their hands around in circular motions and then up and down. A few were doing a version of power walking that I had never seen, and others were doing innovative forms of exercises and isometrics on the sidewalk. Good for them, I thought, as I'd make my way on another sunny day toward the old port city.

I enjoyed seeing the kids going to school and carts led by donkeys in the middle of the road. I smiled as the kids waved to them. When I returned, I took a refreshing dip in the sea and drip-dried on the same blue bench every time. Here my mind turned to Meg as I wondered how she was holding up. *What did she get herself into?* I'd ask myself, always hoping that I'd never get a call from her saying, "I quit!"

I looked on as people with seemingly not a care in the world strolled by in both directions in this cosmopolitan and ancient city. I envied them.

Each day, my thoughts were on Meg and my kids, our puppy Jazz and then on work. I hoped my job would be waiting for me when we arrived home. I yearned to be with the kids and felt that same emptiness I had the last time I came to Israel. So close to them now, yet I hadn't seen them in almost three months. I pictured them running to greet me with arms open wide. Each of us would be talking so fast we'd laugh and have to pause so the other could get a word in.

I tried to fill my time by reading and speaking all the Hebrew I could put my tongue around to prepare for trial and anything else that might come up. Unknown judges, Middle East courts, and a foreign language were all playing havoc on my mind as my phone rang.

David had set up a meeting with Shmuel for the following day. Later than I wanted, but I was looking forward to getting more information regarding my case. I needed time to get used to my surroundings before my court date, and thankfully I was getting more comfortable every day. "How are you doing, Scott?" he asked kindly.

"I'm a bit lonely, nervous and full of falafel." Longing to connect with someone, I continued talking when David, probably sensing I needed a friend, chimed in. "Let's get together for dinner and a chat."

We met later for a bite at a nice Tel Aviv restaurant. David asked, "What are you doing to stay busy?"

"Observing things and being a bit of a tourist too. Did you know that the sand on the beach is very soft and fine, like the west side of Florida? It feels great on my feet."

"Actually, I did. My wife and I take the kids about every two weeks to the beach to swim and play."

We made small talk for a while, and then David grinned. "Let's talk about court and what you'll want to do to prepare. I will meet you at Shmuel's tomorrow at 10 a.m. Is that good for you?"

"Sure. What is our agenda?"

"We'll go over the case and answer any questions you have. We need to file a few more papers as well and may ask for your help to save some money for you." We said good-bye, and once again David picked up the check.

I had time to think as I walked back to my hotel. A garbage strike was now in its second week and the streets reeked. Piles and piles of rancid trash were everywhere and I wondered where they put it all in this small country. I felt safe walking around at night, but in the back of my mind I kept an eye out for anything unusual.

The next morning, I ran along the water again. After taking a dip and stopping at my blue bench, I made my way back to the hotel for some breakfast. I stopped to look at planes as they headed out over the Mediterranean and away from Tel Aviv. Perhaps they were flying home. As they flew out of sight, I thought how badly I desired to be on one of those jets with the kids. I wanted to fly away so badly I could taste it, but I had to remain, trapped until the conclusion of Liza's latest severe lapse in judgment.

Anxious, I arrived at Shmuel's office at 9:30 a.m. As we made our introductions, I could tell that he was a no-nonsense guy. He had black thinning hair, a kind smile, a slight build, and spoke fluent English.

We sat at a big table drinking coffee. "Scott, I am very happy to meet you. I have studied your case carefully both in America and here in Israel. I am impressed by your tenacity and perseverance. I don't think many people would be able to work so hard to be with their children. We are determined to help you reunite with your children. We fully understand what Liza is trying to do and she will fail in the end. Look, on Thursday we will be in court in Tiberius, and I expect to have you reunited with Yonatan and Alexandra."

Realizing he had my full attention, he continued, "Not only that, but I expect that the judge will give you custody until the trial. This is because the court orders from Wisconsin are very specific with regard to the Hague Treaty, which Israel is now a signatory as you know. Unless the judge feels that there is substantial evidence to show that the children would be harmed if placed with you, I believe she will place them with you that day."

"Wow. It's that easy?"

David chimed in, "Well, yes and no. You see, Scott that is the first part. The next steps are very important and will get costly. We need to show the judge at the trial exactly why the children will have to leave their mother in Israel. We will have to educate the judge on The Hague Convention and international child abduction laws. We will need psychological testing and some letters from teachers and friends back home."

"Stop. There's lots of information flowing my way. How much money are we talking here gentlemen, and why the hell do I have to prove all this again and go through what I already did in the States?"

David looked me in the eye. "Around 30,000 U.S. dollars. Look, I know this is tough for you, but there is a lot at stake here and the court needs to be brought up to speed on this.

Also, Liza is going to have two attorneys and they will be fighting to keep the kids here. We must show the court why the children should be placed with you and not stay with their mother."

I shook my head and said softly, "I just want to go home with my children. Why do we need to go to court and have a trial? I already did that! Why more psychological evaluations? Those suckers are tough. Can't the judge look at the rulings from the States where this case has jurisdiction?"

You'd think so, but they told me that certain procedures had to be followed and to me that simply meant more money, no Meg, more time once again lost as a family and no schooling back home for the kids.

The next morning, I drove to Tiberius along the twisting and single lane roads to deliver papers to a gentleman named Moshe. He would have all of the relevant court papers from the U.S. filed in the court for the judge, as they had already been translated. I felt apprehensive as I entered the town I had last left veiled in a lie.

Now nearing the lion's den, I kept thinking that someone would notice me and tell Liza. Looking in my rearview mirror, I noticed a police car with flashing blue lights coming up fast. My heart sinking, I held my breath and watched as it closed in, and then passed me.

Moshe and I met at a gas station near the city. We spoke for a few minutes, and he assured me that the papers would be taken directly to the courthouse to be filed. The very same courthouse that sat connected to the police station where two of Liza's brothers worked. I thanked him, hopped into my car, and headed back to Tel Aviv.

September 6 started with a bang, as car bombs went off in Haifa and Tiberius. My thoughts went immediately to Jonathan and Alexandra. *Are they safe?* I wondered. *Who is keeping an eye on them?*

I feared for them and hoped that they were okay. Unnerving me to the core, I stayed away from most public places that day and hunkered down in my hotel room. The news stations all had reporters sadly showing footage of mangled cars, destroyed shops, and dead and injured civilians. My first time being so close to this carnage, I wanted to call Meg for comfort, but thought better of it. She had enough on her plate, and I didn't want to add to it.

I had dozed off when my phone rang. I answered and Shmuel began straight away. "Scott, Liza's attorneys went to the judge requesting to postpone the September 9th court date." I listened, while my heart sank. "But do not worry. The judge denied their request and we are still scheduled for that day. Liza's attorneys are aware that they will have to hand the children over to you and are trying to avoid that."

"Shmuel, I am trying to keep it together, but between my situation, car bombs, lawyers, and courts, I'm a bit freaked out. My children are entangled in an international custody case. I'm far from home and I don't have them with me. Thanks for the update. Please keep my case as your top priority."

"Scott, I want you to know that my business is good, but I am also a father. What I am saying is that I know that this is important to you and it is also to me. It is getting much of my attention, I assure you."

Possible delays, worrying about the children, and thinking about Meg back home tested my resolve, but I continued moving forward in a country where things often move painfully slow.

Now paranoid because of the latest bombings, I imagined people watching me as I went about my business. Perhaps I overreacted, but I was in the Middle East where anything and everything often happens in a split second. Looking for comfort, I grabbed a beer and said to myself, "The court date stands firm. Score one for the good guys!"

The next day, I walked down the street near the Dizengoff center when a couple approached me, asking for directions in Hebrew. I understood some of what they were saying and knew the city pretty well so I could help them find their destination. Impressed and slightly surprised by this, I began to feel more like I fit in.

Since Liza now knew that I was in Israel, I called her to ask to speak with the children. No reason to get into an argument with her, but I listened for three minutes while she spoke her mind. "Why did you have to come here? You should be at work or with your wife, shouldn't you? There's no way in the world you're getting the kids, Scott. Go home. The children are happy here and don't need you around, so you'd better go home. Don't bother coming here because the kids are busy and won't have time for you," she continued in front of our son as she passed the phone to him.

"Dad, I love you, but we are staying here," he said in an uncharacteristically stern tone.

"No, you're not, my love. We will be heading home soon, sweetheart, and I am so sorry for all of the confusion. I know it must hurt you, but this is what must happen."

He said nothing for a moment and then broke the silence. "Do you want to speak with Ally?"

"Yes, I do, sweetie. I love you a lot."

"Hi, Daddy. I don't want to go either and you can't make us because mom said so. Why don't you just go home and we'll write you. I promise."

No doubt their mom said so. What a waste of energy and desperation on her part. Telling this to our children again and again only fed into her sad reality, which was no reality at all.

"Ally, I need you to think about your friends back home. Think about your room and Meg, too. I know she misses you and Jazz does, too. We will be going back soon and I am so sorry for any pain this has caused you, my love."

"I have to go now, Dad. Bye."

Now fuming, even Israelis with their tough exterior and bold attitudes would have done well to keep their distance from me at that point.

How quickly Liza had turned them against me, and I hated her for doing so. Moreover, she had the chance to be kind and gentle with their minds and souls, as Meg and I were, and instead treated them like clay toys to be molded into her own demented version of reality. Meg continued to be the one person protected from Liza's bashing. The children trusted her and were growing to love her. They must have known deep down that this woman was the real deal. Perhaps sensing this, Liza continued being careful not to attack her.

I went back to my hotel to calm down. Meg and I had worked so hard and Liza quickly began breaking down many of the positive strides we had made.

I called and spoke to Meg at work. I explained what had occurred in court and the present mental state of the kids. "It's so good to hear from you," she said. "I'm sorry that you have to go through such hell, but I think that things are going to be fine in the end. Are you being safe and watching your back?"

"Yes, babe, I am watching my back and am preparing myself once again for the battle ahead. How are you holding up? How is Jazz doing?"

"I'm fine, but this is really tough. Work, the home, and a new puppy along with the three of you being gone is a lot for me to handle."

I wasn't about to share with her the most recent car bombings nor the healthy amount of fear coursing through my body. "I'm getting angry and this is good. I'm still focused, but I feel like kicking some ass in court. I wonder if I can have a translator during the proceedings. I'd feel lost if they only spoke Hebrew."

"You'll have to ask David, but I would think they'd allow that. I miss you a lot. Do you miss me?"

"A little, I suppose, but these Israeli women are hot."

"Ha ha ha, very funny. I know you are being a good boy."

"Can't fool you, even from this distance." I laughed. "I miss you so much and really would love to be holding you right now."

We spoke longer and agreed to talk every day or two. I knew she was worried with my being far away in this land shrouded in mystery and chaos, so I tried to comfort her every time we spoke. In doing so, it helped to keep my fear to a manageable level as well. Tiberius would be my next challenge. They would come at me like never before, trying to weaken my resolve and destroy my life.

◆ ◆ ◆

CHAPTER 22

BACK IN THE LION'S DEN

◆◆◆

I ARRIVED ALONE the day of court and waited for David and Shmuel before showing my face. I had a healthy dose of trepidation and wanted as little commotion as possible.

Sitting outside on a bench I watched as police with guns ushered people in handcuffs to jail. Plenty of other folks walked around, smoking, and waiting. A cinematic version of life unfolded before my eyes. Colorful people and not-so-familiar surroundings took me to a dream-like state. I had to nudge myself to regain focus and remember where I was.

I spotted my attorneys exiting Shmuel's car. We caught up and talked outside in the shade.

Also outside in street clothes, waiting to say hello, were Liza's brothers, Danny and Shimon. The three of us had gone shooting in the hills outside Tiberius a few years back. They sported their pistols at their sides as they approached.

I hoped I'd be okay surrounded by so many eyes, but I stood defenseless in a small city with two of its police officers not so happy with me. My first thought was to turn quickly and walk away.

Shimon yelled my name. "Scotty, how are you doing, man?" Both hugged me and gave me a kiss on each cheek.

"Good to see you," I said, hoping to avoid a scene.

"Look Scott, we are sorry for Liza's behavior," Danny said. "It is not good for the kids, and I know you're a good father. We saw Yoni and Ally and they are fine. They miss you and Meg. They really like her. So good luck with this and take care."

This surprised me. "Nothing personal," I said to them with a half- smile and a healthy dose of caution. "I'm doing what I must to be with my children. How are your parents?"

"They are fine. Mom misses you, but Dad is upset. He doesn't think Liza did anything wrong because he wants the kids here."

"Don't worry, Scotty. We miss you and wish that none of this was happening. I hope that we can see you again, my brother," Shimon said.

Nice to hear, I suppose. We hugged again and said a final good-bye. I focused on the unknown waiting for me inside the building. My attorneys and I entered the courthouse and, as we did, I saw Liza standing by the security line, smiling and talking to people I did not recognize.

She looked worn down, as if life had taken more than just a bite out of her. We exchanged nods as I walked into court with my attorneys. In the front of the small room there stood a large raised platform. Judge Esther Bohadana would be presiding. Liza's attorneys, Marsella Bochbut and Pamela Butter, would represent the children. Although American-born, Butter and I didn't hit it off. The tension felt awkward. She stared at me, trying to size me up. I did the same and waited until she broke eye contact.

Hebrew was being spoken in the courtroom, so I only picked up parts of the discussions flowing around me as the judge entered the room. Petite with shoulder-length, brown hair, her black robe almost enveloped her. She had a pleasant smile and demeanor and appeared to be sharp as she spoke in English and Hebrew. She laid down the ground rules for the day and made sure that everyone understood that today we were there to deal with the temporary placement of the children, not trial-related issues. When she finished, I raised my hand. "Yes, Mr. Lesnick?" she said, kindly.

"Judge, my Hebrew is limited and I don't want to miss anything that is being said. Can I have a translator to help me understand what is being said?"

"I'm sorry, but that is not permitted. You will have to get information from your attorneys as we proceed. I will permit them to speak quietly to you or write down anything they want from this point on."

I pressed my case. "Your Honor, does that not put me at a disadvantage? There is much at stake and I may need to add something to what is being said by either side."

"I understand, Mr. Lesnick, but there will not be a translator. Your attorneys will have to fill you in when they think it is necessary."

David could tell that I was pissed and about to speak again when he put his hand on mine to stop me from crossing a line and possibly hurting my chances. Shmuel looked at me and closed his eyes for a second while shaking his head. I got the message: move on and let them do their jobs.

The judge called me to the stand and I prepared for a grilling from the dark side. It didn't take long for me to realize that no chair would be provided. I pointed this out by asking if I was to stand or did they simply forget the chair.

"You will be standing, Mr. Lesnick," the judge said. So stand I did. At first, it felt like an interrogation without the handcuffs, the kind that we witness on television. The accused dictator stands on trial for crimes against humanity in the maximum security courtroom. I would wind up standing without a break for almost three hours.

As the last words were leaving the judge's mouth, a cell phone went off, and the look on her face was one of disbelief. After rummaging around in her purse for five rings, Liza finally turned it off. The judge appeared visibly annoyed.

Pam Butter began and it became obvious to me at the start from her body language and aggressive demeanor that she was determined to rattle me. I had faced and defeated Larry years before, so I remained remarkably calm and tough under her non-stop barrage of questions and accusations. She accused me of many wrongdoings back in the States of which she claimed to have proof. I knew she didn't and that the accusations were false. Bullying me would not work as I remained focused on my children.

"Why do you want to take the children from their mother? You told Liza that she was a better parent than you were. Is that not true? Have you hit your children on many occasions? How many times did you hit Liza? Isn't it true that you cheated on Liza on several occasions? Why did you spend so much time away from your children? Do you really believe that you're fit enough to raise Yonatan and Alexandra? What would you say if I told you that your children would rather live in Israel with their mother?"

I responded each time with strong rebukes of all of her statements. "They are *our* children, not hers. I did not kidnap them; your clients' mother did. I am a far better parent than Liza, and no, I do not hit them nor did I ever hit Liza. As to your allegations that I cheated on Liza, it would be most difficult to prove because I never did. I'm offended that you would say such a thing, Ms. Butter. Have you seen her psychological evaluation from the U.S.?"

I glanced back and forth between David and Shmuel often to make sure they were okay with my speaking the truth that way. They were, and I never once looked Pam in the eyes as she often tried to stare me down.

Shmuel interjected when needed. It appeared that the judge usually sided with him. As I continued to answer questions and state my position to all things related to the case, I began to tear up. I spoke of the children and the extremely rough road they had traveled. I went on to tell how Liza manipulated me and the courts to get what she wanted, putting our children in psychological danger, at the very least. I felt angry, hurt and beleaguered as I attempted to drive my points home in the only language I could. Butter sat in her chair saying nothing. I remained steadfast in my determination to bring my children back to America for good.

When she finished, I had 40 minutes more from Liza's attorney, Miss Bochbut, without a break. I did my best to give her nothing as she repeated some of the same questions Butter asked, attempting to trip me up. Although tired, I stood my ground.

I would not allow these ladies to stand in the way of my reuniting with my children, as Liza had attempted to do on two previous occasions. Highly focused, I did not let these two push me around. I felt more relaxed than I had expected, which allowed me to have some control during their intense cross-examination. They finally finished up, and the judge permitted me to go the bathroom and relax for 15 minutes.

When we returned to the courtroom, Shmuel asked me some questions under oath that showed the court why the children should be with me, and then he wrapped up.

It would be Liza's turn next.

I was dismissed and we took a much-needed break for lunch. David hugged me. "Scott, you did fine up there. Anything they might have been looking for, you didn't give them. I think Butter crossed the line several times. This will not help their case."

"After lunch, Liza will take the stand. I imagine she will get low and accuse you of things that she cannot prove. It is our belief that the judge will not put much weight in her rants as they have little bearing on the case. We are well prepared for her and I am looking forward to getting her up there."

After eating and relaxing, the three of us walked the short distance back to the courthouse, where people milled around outside. Suddenly, Liza's father, Joseph, approached us. He looked older than when we last said goodbye and not at all happy. He yelled, "Scott, you lied to me. I want you to leave the children here and go home. You are a bad father." Walking away, I told him to leave me alone. He took a swing at me.

I moved out of the way and said angrily, "Joseph, you should be furious with Liza, not me. I gave her many opportunities, and she ruined our marriage. As a father and a grandfather you behaved poorly."

He continued to yell obscenities until one of his sons came to get him. As he walked away I said, "Hey Joseph. Your daughter is a liar and you should be ashamed of yourself for supporting such behavior. I expected better from you."

Shmuel and David ushered me back toward the courthouse for the afternoon session. Not much harm but plenty of action had occurred this day in the cozy seaside town of Tiberius.

Liza was grilled, and I do mean grilled to the point of *well done*, by Shmuel for one hour and forty-five minutes.

She had always been her own worst enemy and her numerous past actions brought to the attention of the judge spoke volumes. She was not able to keep friends, not able to keep a job, she lied under oath. Also, she kidnapped my children, twice. In the middle of her testimony, Liza asked the judge if she could take a break for a cigarette. The judge denied her request and my team continued to dissect her testimony.

Shmuel finished by reading the findings of the psychologist who had tested Liza and me in the States.

The reading of the psychologist's report proved powerful as David slipped me a note. It read: "Shmuel has devastated their case and the judge knows this. Liza is not doing well and I sense she's aware of this, too."

After a brief 15 minute recess, we returned to hear the judge's verdict. We rose as she entered the room and took her seat on the bench. Thankfully she gave her ruling in English.

"The children and all of their belongings are to be placed with their father within two-hours' time as they are nearby. The switch will take place there at the police station."

Liza and her attorneys objected, but the decision had come down. Once again I would be reunited with Jonathan and Alexandra. I could not have been happier. Ecstatic and overcome with emotion, I remained silent.

Liza, on the other hand, appeared to be beyond livid and yelled at the judge. I expected nothing less.

◆◆◆

CHAPTER 23

REUNITED AT LAST

◆◆◆

OUR TRIAL DATE was set for September 29, 1999. My lawyers asked me to stay away from Tiberius, given the unusual circumstances. I spent the next twenty days schooling Jonathan and Ally. We also had hands-on history lessons as we visited some of the country's rich historical sites.

Since I had anticipated this outcome, I had come prepared with some reading, math, and other materials at the appropriate grade level. The ride to Tel Aviv was quiet at first, and then the questions began. Jonathan had many of them. "Dad, when are we going to see Mom? Do you have to do more court or are we going home? Why are we with you now? Mom said the judge made a mistake and we would be with her soon. Who can I speak with to fix this?"

Great questions deserved thoughtful answers so we stopped outside of Tel Aviv far enough away from Tiberius for food and something to drink.

The judge had taken the kids aside after our proceedings to tell them what would happen and why she made the decision to have them go with me. They were not thrilled, but since the judge, a neutral party, had told them in Hebrew, it appeared to carry some weight. I explained that we needed to return to Milwaukee, as school had begun and I needed to get back to work.

"Look, I know how hard and awkward this must be for the two of you, and I am so sorry. I love you both so much. That is why I came here. I am only doing what the judge in America and the judge here in Israel told me to do. We will call your mom tomorrow and you can speak as long as you want. There will be more court at the end of the month. We are going to have to see another psychologist here, like we did in Milwaukee. After that, your mother and I will go to court and hear their final decision. Meg and I think that you are both wonderful children and need stability in your lives. We are going to give you that, I promise." I could tell they were less than thrilled with my explanation, but they had grown to know that I would be honest with them.

The court had put this case on a fast track because it involved child abduction and the Hague Treaty. Otherwise, my attorneys advised me, we would have been waiting many months to see a judge, just like in the States. Now looking at 30 days or more before I could possibly go home with my kids, I knew I'd need to remain flexible.

The children's passports had a hold on them and I wasn't going home without them. Passport control would not allow them to exit the country until the courts removed the hold.

I moved out of my hotel for larger quarters and anonymity, not wanting Liza or anyone connected with her to know our exact location. I placed a call to Meg, who was thrilled to learn that the children were now with me. I sensed ease in their voices as they spoke with her on the phone. Our new puppy had become a big topic for them. They wanted to make sure he was okay. It energized us all to speak with Meg, as her calm voice and level head were just what we all needed. She called my manager at work to update him as well.

On September 10, 1999, the four of us had our first meeting with the court-appointed psychologist. While the kids were in another room reading, Liza proceeded to yell loudly at Dr. Gotleib on a number of topics. Some weren't even related to our case. She got quite animated and wild as I sat back watching and listening to her rant. I kept my mouth shut unless asked a specific question.

Jonathan and Ally saw him separately. Feeling so worn out afterward, I could barely negotiate the winding streets back to our hotel. Watching my back and the children's while staying focused presented problems as well. I remember thinking, *I'm tired of this country and want my life back.* The children needed stability as well, and I wasn't sure when Meg and I would be allowed to provide it for them. Keeping them occupied each day and not fighting proved to be a chore. Jonathan maintained his young expert's rating at pushing the boundaries I set for him. He also pushed Ally's buttons. Not being at home in Milwaukee, their unknown future, and missing their mother added additional stress.

The next day we decided to visit the Tel Aviv Art Museum to see a great exhibit by Columbian painter Fernando Botero. We laughed and enjoyed life. For a while, we forgot where we were. After some culture and a swim in the ocean, we were able to relax and overlook our troubles.

That evening, Jonathan once again began pushing Ally's buttons. I couldn't parent at full capacity because we were going to visit the psychologist again in one day. I feared that even giving him a time out might be mentioned during the interviews. I knew he had a lot of pressure building up, but I had to keep some semblance of control. He'd left our room without telling me, bugged his sister until she yelled or cried, and refused to follow directions. I knew he had shouldered the brunt of his mother's cerebral and verbal assaults and I felt so bad for him. However, I had to keep things together and him under control if the three of us were going to survive alone on the road.

Three days after our first appointment, the children and I arrived at Dr. Gotleib's office with time to spare. Liza arrived 25 minutes late.

Each of us saw the doctor separately. Liza and I also had another joint session in which she acted somewhat more subdued. I listened to this, the woman I had once loved and had now grown to hate, continue to act as if the world owed her something.

Dr. Gotleib proved difficult but not impossible to read. I saw his concern over Liza's state of mind and lack of concern for mine. I knew I wasn't nuts, just a normal person under immense stress trying to do the right thing for his children. No harm there, yet plenty of harm for Liza. I once again allowed myself to be mentally poked and prodded, which left me exhausted.

When we finished, I walked out of the office with the children and without Liza.

"Daddy, can we go see a movie?" Ally asked.

"When the two of you finish your homework, I'll take you out to dinner and a movie."

"Can we see *Wild, Wild West* with Will Smith?" Jonathan asked.

"Yes we can big guy. Now let's get back to our hotel so you can do your math, please."

After the movie we took a late swim. Jonathan kept pushing his sister around as big brothers sometimes do, and she began to scream. He would not listen to my repeated attempts to stop from my chair so I went into the pool, grabbed his shoulders and said, "Look, I know that this has been difficult for you and Ally, but you are making it harder on all of us. I know you are under a lot of pressure, my love, but I need you to help me out now more than ever by staying as grounded as you can. Please know that I will punish you here in Israel just as I would back home if you do this again. You must practice better self-control. Are we clear on this?"

"Yes, Dad."

"Good. Now leave your sister alone."

We headed up to our room, and I phoned Meg. We were both worn out with worry and financial stress. I had to pay $975 to the good doctor for his services and the same to cover Liza's portion. Paying the money for her—the very principle of it—hurt a lot. I could still leave Israel at any time; they just wouldn't continue the testing and interviews without being paid first. Liza pleaded poverty.

I also awaited another bill from our attorneys. My total hotel bills had reached $3,000, which I paid every week. Our clothes were all dirty, and I had been doing laundry at a local laundromat to stay on top of things. Liza had given me only half of their clothes, so we bought some more underwear and shirts. I switched hotels again following the advice of my attorneys.

This would make it nearly impossible to serve me with any papers. Liza and her attorney remained on the warpath.

I wondered if a ten and twelve year old could comprehend what enormous steps I'd taken on their behalf, but it really didn't matter since I had decided how far I was willing to go for them years ago.

Later, Jonathan called his mother. He mentioned that we had gone swimming and that I had grabbed his neck to choke him. I understood he was torn apart by his present situation, but I had a job to do before Meg and I could once again begin to repair the damage heaped upon his sister and him. His mother called social services and within a few hours we heard a knock on our door. Jonathan must have told Liza where we were.

"Mr. Lesnick?" Two women stood at the door.

"Yes. Who are you?"

"We are with children's social services. Can we talk to you outside? There has been a complaint about you choking your son and we're here to investigate."

I took all of five seconds to compose myself and listened carefully to what they had to say in disbelief. I attempted to explain what had happened and the situation we were all in.

They listened to my heartfelt explanation and took plenty of notes. I sensed that they were checking into things, yet didn't seem overly concerned. Apparently, they were satisfied with my answers and the weary look on my face, and said that no further details were needed. They wished me good luck. I never heard from them again.

A near-death experience while still being conscious is the best way I can describe how I felt during this latest grilling. I couldn't really blame my son, because his mother had thrown so much on his little shoulders. On the contrary, I felt so bad for his pain and suffering. I blamed myself for getting him and his sister into this awful situation, but I still had enough fight in me to try to correct it.

Being in limbo and living in one room continued getting to us, and having a cold just made matters worse.

That night we had dinner with others. It felt nice to be around other friendly people. We talked to families from the U.S., England, Australia, Russia, and Germany. The kids had a rare opportunity to spend some time with children their own age, which seemed to help recharge them.

Now September 15, the day Dr. Gotleib would give his recommendations, I sat by my phone waiting for it to ring. On pins and needles, I had to smile because the children didn't realize how intense things were. I shielded them from much of the details, hoping that they'd have less internal stress. Even with the beautiful runs I took in the morning, my stress levels were high.

David had called every few days to check in, and I knew that he'd soon contact me with the results from our psychological examination. Both kids were watching *The Nanny* on TV and laughing when he called. I told the children I would be outside and left the room for privacy. My heart raced and I had difficulty catching my breath.

David sounded excited. "Scott, first of all, I want to tell you that I have just finished reading Dr. Gotleib's report. It is all in our favor, which is huge for us. You know, I am not surprised after knowing you and getting to know Liza." Thrilled to hear the great news and overwhelmed by all of the pain and suffering the children, Meg and I had endured, I let out a huge sigh.

I paused to think for a moment and began to cry, a huge and cleansing cry. So many thoughts spanning 15 years rushed through my mind. It became apparent to me that I was under more stress than I realized.

Composing myself I said, "Thank you so much for all of your help. Your heart is big and your skills, combined with Shmuel's, are saving my family. I just want you to know that I am aware of it."

"Scott, I don't think that I would have the mental and physical drive to do what you have done. It is amazing, and I am proud to know you. My life has been touched by you, and I appreciate your honesty, courage, and strength, my friend."

"Wow, normally I'd have some funny line to say back, but I think I'm just going to say thank you."

"We have more to do and I will call you tomorrow. Get some rest and enjoy your kids."

"I will. Please give my thanks to Shmuel, also." I walked back into the room feeling weak. The children noticed that I had been crying and asked if everything was all right. "I'm fine. It has just been a long bunch of weeks. Let's go get some dinner."

On September 16, 1999, I was back in court in Tiberius for Pam Butter's cross-examination of Dr. Gotleib's report. Once again, people were being ushered around in handcuffs, and blaring sirens played havoc on my frayed nerves. I noticed many people wearing sandals, which made me jealous. I wore my nice black dress shoes and had ironed my shirt that morning.

The sun baked the sidewalks and the humidity was relentless. I walked over to a man standing under a tree with a cart of cold sodas and food. He appeared to be doing brisk business. I bought a Coke and headed toward the courthouse. I felt a long way from home and was cranky and nervous as I once again walked through the courthouse door. David and Shmuel were there and we spoke briefly before entering the courtroom.

Once again, Butter came out aggressively, as she had the doctor on the stand for almost two hours. He stated in his report that "the best interest of the minors required that they return immediately to the USA."

I had difficulty understanding most of the dialogue. Shmuel assured me that Butter was getting nowhere. When she turned away from the judge, I would smile right into Butter's dark eyes.

I sensed her annoyance at my childish behavior. She continued to be relentless, as if my children had it much better with a twice professionally diagnosed damaged mother. Finally, she completed her cross-examination. The doctor, unperturbed, said a few words to David before leaving.

We had a short recess. Upon our return, and to everyone's surprise, the judge simply asked Liza to let the children go back to America. Thrilled that she made this statement, I hoped this gigantic mess would end that moment.

Liza predictably said, "No."

The judge asked for closing arguments. Shmuel went first. He appeared eloquent as the judge listened carefully to him. I could understand about a quarter of his words, but his body language crossed all dialects. Speaking slowly and with passion, I watch as the judge soaked in every word. Next up was the other side. The judge listened to them carefully as well and then finally, to my relief, both sides rested. When I walked outside to get the kids, I hugged Shmuel and David. No words were said. None were needed.

I got the hell out of there and headed back to our hotel outside of Tel Aviv with the kids. The staff knew us pretty well by now, and we had fun with them. They were curious, as were others we met along the way, as to why the children were not in school. I'd told people that we were on an Israel discovery tour as part of their home-schooling program. I spoke highly of the country I couldn't wait to leave, and the questions subsided.

Now Monday, September 20, 1999, I had been stuck here for three weeks, which also meant three weeks of not working. Things were fine back home, or as fine as our situation allowed. Meg held down the fort and answered the barrage of questions that kept coming her way from family and friends. I had the kids doing math and reading every day in what we called "hotel school."

Jonathan suffered and still wanted to stay with his mother. Understandably, he hoped for an ending that brought the four of us back together as one happy family. I had difficulty dealing with his erratic behavior. Aware of his many gifts and intelligence, I often reminded him how talented and special Meg and I thought he was.

Ally had it hard, too. I knew she hurt, and giving hugs to both of them while sprinkling praise was common throughout every day. I reminded her of her beautiful red hair and how so many people loved it. We talked about her many talents, which included problem-solving and not choosing sides between her mother and me. I praised her often for trying so hard to keep it together.

As our money dwindled away, the hotel room seemed to get smaller by the day. But I realized that I had accomplished a lot since my arrival. The children were with me, and Liza no longer had their passports. I had spent tens of thousands of dollars, and thankfully, the psychological report came back in our favor.

The following day David called to check in and go over my bill. I owed him $20,000 above and beyond the $15,000 I had already paid. He didn't pressure me and I told him I would work on it.

I called Meg and apologized for all she had to go through. She continued to be her normal strong self and helped me remain that way as well. I mentioned the money and David's request for more funds, and we decided to have her make a tough call to our close friends, Andy and Linda, who were well off financially. Although we hated to ask, they agreed to help us out. Very kind of them, it made a huge difference in our mental state. Eventually, we paid them back in full with a little extra and many thanks.

David called the next day. "Scott, we have an issue. Liza's attorney called to notify me that they would appeal any decision that is not favorable to them. This could mean more money and months of proceedings. Shmuel and I are meeting later today to discuss options. We will call you back soon. Don't worry yet, my friend. They are positioning themselves for a big fall and I don't think the courts will allow the children to stay in limbo too long. The judge will make her ruling on the 29th of this month."

"Thanks, I guess. David, I don't have an unlimited amount of time and money. Things are difficult and I am completely worn out. I need to get the children home and in school soon. That is my top priority, so when the two of you get together, please make that the goal."

The days moved at a snail's pace, and the kids were climbing the walls. I tried hard to keep them occupied, but I knew that the solution was for us to be home.

I spoke to Meg, who began to show signs of suffering, too. The stress got to everyone, and young Jonathan continued to behave poorly. Ally suffered too, so I would take them for long walks around Tel Aviv and along the ocean. *I can't imagine what they're going through*, I thought.

As we made our way back from the ocean, we heard loud noises and music coming down one of the major streets. The Love Parade was in full swing and thousands of people of all ages were having a blast. There were floats, cars, and bicycles, all decorated. People were in costumes as well, and drugs and alcohol were being used freely. The police kept a watchful eye as men and women of all ages let go of most or all of their inhibitions. The kids enjoy the spectacle as much as I did. After 45 minutes, we headed toward our hotel. We walked along a large outdoor market and bought some food to take back.

One day we decided to go to Jerusalem. As we walked around the Old City, I let the kids test their bargaining skills at the different stores and with vendors. Jonathan proved to be a natural, and I stood back to let him have some much-needed fun. Impressed by his confidence, Ally and I followed him as he proceeded to weave in and out of shops and narrow alleys. A bit shy, Ally eventually enjoyed talking to the kind people in their small stores. A few hours of unusual smells and sights did us good. I continued to allow them to lead while I kept an eye on where we were.

I showed them a secret set of stairs that led above the market. We walked on roofs and peeked in a few windows. "Are we allowed to be up here, Dad?" Ally asked.

Before I could answer, Jonathan chimed in, "Sure Ally, it's okay."

We walked more and then took the same stairs back down.

The evening of September 28 could not have been tougher. The kids were tired of the hotel and we'd all had enough of one another. We went to bed early to get plenty of rest. Tomorrow was Decision Day.

◆ ◆ ◆

CHAPTER 24

DECISION DAY

◆◆◆

I ROLLED OUT of bed and woke the kids. They each took a shower and proceeded to get dressed. Next, I made sure the water in the shower was cold. I needed to feel alive and refreshed for the ride to court.

We drove to Tiberius in record time. I entered the closed session courtroom while the children spent time with their grandparents outside. This was a foreign country, and I was reminded of it every moment. The customs, language, the Hebrew writing, and different but beautiful landscapes reminded me that I was still far from home and U.S. courts—the same courts that had already awarded me primary placement of Jonathan and Alexandra.

Nervous, I decided to pull out the one pack of lucky Tic Tacs I had brought from home. Popping one into my mouth comforted me as I greeted Shmuel and David with a half-hearted smile.

David put his arm around my shoulder as the more reserved Shmuel asked how I was holding up. "I'm hanging in there, gentlemen. Did you get the $20,000 Meg sent?"

"Yes, we did. Thank you."

I kept hearing the Beatles' tune, "Getting Better All the Time" in my head. I always loved their music, and the song helped to relax me as we approached the table where we had already sat several times. Once situated, I let them talk as I zoned out with my make-believe Sony Walkman. Liza and her attorneys, all dressed in black, were the next to arrive.

Judge Esther Bohadana entered a few minutes later, already knowing our fate. She had met with the children privately before our session to explain her decision and how it would affect them. I wanted to be there to comfort them no matter what her decision, but procedure took precedence over parenting.

Judge Bohadana had a lot to say and was kind enough to speak in English. She left no doubt that much time and careful consideration went into her decision. Here is some of what she said:

While with the children in Israel in 1999, the mother took them to a legal aid office in Haifa. On July 12, 1999, the mother took the minors to see a psychologist.

On August 11, 1999, a judge gave Liza an injunction to prohibit the father from returning the children to the U.S.

A hearing was set for August 15, 1999, and Liza was to notify me of this. I was never informed of it. Carefully coached by lawyers, Liza had the children initiate these legal moves to stay in Israel, therefore, did not commit an actual act of "abduction".

When arriving in Israel, I filed my claim with the central authority of the Hague Convention in the USA and requested its assistance in returning the minors. (She continued, stating in a louder voice that all claims other than the father's were far-fetched.) *On September 9, 1999 it was agreed to dismiss the two files for temporary orders. And the court had only the father's request according to the Hague Law to act upon.*

Claims of violence by the father to the minors were not well-based and sounded like a repetition of things the children were told to memorize for court. Time after time, experts in the USA and Israel rejected the claims regarding the father and physical or psychological harm to the minors. (She went on to say that the children repeat what the mother tells them.) *The father may have yelled or spanked on occasion, but nothing more.*

Her conclusions were as follows: the children were to be returned to the father's custody at once. She granted her permission to me to return to the States with Jonathan and Alexandra the next day.

Needless to say, I was overjoyed and filled with emotions both positive and not so positive. I knew that this would be very hard for my kids and I felt terrible for putting them through this. She appointed the social worker who'd seen the children before I arrived to help make a smooth transition.

The children's passports, being held by the secretary in Tiberius, were to go immediately to Shmuel, who would give them to me. The stay-of-exit order, which had prohibited me from leaving the country with Jonathan and Alexandra, would be canceled.

Again, we were victorious and thrilled while Liza and her team tried in vain to interrupt the judge mid-sentence and change her mind. Border police would be informed of the decision by the court at once.

Per the judge's order, Liza could talk to the children on the phone before they left.

And the kicker, my second dream come true, was that Liza was ordered to pay *all* of my expenses totaling $45,000! I had wanted her to pay, and now I had the legal means to make her.

I gave both of my attorneys a bear hug and thanked them for their guidance and help.

Liza, spit flying from her mouth, was furious and demanded to speak with the judge. No conversation took place, however. I smiled at Liza and she muttered something I chose to ignore.

◆ ◆ ◆

CHAPTER 25
OH, COME ON!

◆◆◆

SEPTEMBER 30, 1999 should have been the day the three of us headed back to the States but, as warned by Liza's attorneys after the judge's verdict, Liza appealed the court's decision, putting me in yet another difficult position.

It would take even more time and money. The children would miss yet more school. My "hotel schooling" did not meet the standards Meg and I had set for them and they needed to be home and away from their mother's caustic grasp.

More days passed. I had been gone from work for five weeks and feared losing my job. Although I had spoken to Meg the day before to give her the great news, I decided it was time to call her again. "You may have to come home and leave the kids there until the appeal is over," she said sadly. "I need you and I miss you. Work needs you and we cannot afford much more of this. Liza will never pay us the $45,000 anyway, so that order from the court will never turn into money."

Now in a not-so-mild panic, I yelled, "Babe, we've come so far and I refuse to leave without the children. There must be another way. There always is. In my eyes, we will have failed the children if I fly home without them."

Just then the hotel phone rang. The kids were in the lobby waiting for me. Moshe, an Israeli psychologist who had seen Liza and the kids before anyone notified me of this travesty, was on the line.

I told Meg that I would call her back soon and took Moshe's call. He asked me to negotiate with Liza, "Scott, the children should be with both parents and they need their mother. I will be happy to see both you and Liza to discuss this further. When can we meet?"

"Moshe, the woman you're speaking about abandoned her children and moved half a world away. And I will add that you're being rather presumptuous thinking you can force yourself into another man's personal life." I went on to tell the bastard to mind his own business and stay away from my children. I further told him that if he ever tried to contact me again, I'd call the police in Tel Aviv at once.

I slammed down the phone and headed downstairs a bit shaken, once again trying to keep a brave face in front of the kids.

I called Meg back and both Jonathan and Alexandra said hello to her. They chatted for twenty minutes about home, their friends, and our dog and then handed the phone back to me. I wanted to sit and talk to Meg for an hour, but only had ten minutes. We were continually helping each other stay strong by encouraging the other to think of good times. Picking up our puppy for the first time made us laugh and smile, and we joked about how she was alone to train him. Remembering the good times with the kids and our family picnics helped ease the tension, too. We said our goodbyes and hugged each other tightly over the phone.

We again changed hotels to avoid being served with papers. A real-life drama of hide-and-seek. This time I kept a closer eye on Jonathan so that he would not disclose our new location in Be'er Sheva. Once again, we checked into a hotel where we were complete strangers. The spacious two rooms and queen beds provided the three of us some extra needed elbow room.

Shmuel phoned me as we were unpacking. "Scott, we might need you at the appellate court in Nazareth tomorrow. We will have to educate the judge about the Hague Convention because he knows nothing about it. Do you know where Nazareth is?"

"Everyone knows that one. It's in the Holy Land."

"Yes, it is," he said, getting my humor, but not laughing. "Do you know how to get there if we need you?"

"Yes."

"We have a court date set for October 11, which is coming up very fast and in accordance with the guidelines of the Convention. They are trying to appeal, which means you cannot leave, Scott. We need you here. I am going to try very hard with David to change this and get you and your children home earlier."

"Okay. Let me know."

I was exhausted. Foreign lands and courts were taking their toll on me emotionally and physically.

The next day, David and Shmuel were in the Nazareth Court of Appeals for most of the morning. They did not need me there, so I hung out at a pool with the kids and tried to relax; pacing, wondering when my days in Israel would be over.

My cash low, my morale continued to be chipped away as our fate lay in a state of flux. I worried how I would be able to continue protecting the kids. Paranoia crept in; I was sure that someone was watching us. Ready to give my life for Jonathan and Ally, I stood willing to fight off anyone who came my way with a make-believe reservoir of testosterone and karate moves.

Continuing to watch the kids, I reminded myself that I needed to keep my act together and forced myself to remain focused in the present. My mind was still intact, but, oh, the games I allowed it to play. "They need you to be strong," I kept telling myself. "Stay focused. You never know what's around the corner."

That afternoon, the kids were resting in our room when the phone rang. David was on the other end, speaking a thousand miles a minute.

"Shmuel and I met in front of Judge Hatib Hashem here in Nazareth and he has done his homework. I was very impressed with his understanding of all that has transpired. They had six different lawyers to our two and the courtroom exploded with noise. It was an incredible scene, and I wish you could have been here. We were yelling and they were yelling and the judge did his best to keep things from completely spiraling out of control. Anyway, my friend, after reading all of the material presented to him and applying the law as he saw it, his decision was to cancel his recent stay order. He is allowing you and the children to leave at once! Are you still listening, Scott? Scott?"

I placed my head in my hand and let out a huge sigh. Just 24 hours earlier we were looking at spending much more time and money, and now it appeared that I'd be free to go home with my children. Could this really be true? Would I soon be on one of those planes with Jonathan and Alexandra? I so coveted the jets as I watched them after my runs, flying over the sea and heading west to America.

"I'm here, David. I am so incredibly thrilled and very thankful to you and Shmuel. Does this really mean that I can go home to Milwaukee with them?"

"Look, Scott, there's more. The judge noted that the continuation of the delay of implementation of Judge Bohadana's decision would cause much harm to the children and to you, in contrast to the inconvenience of Liza if there would be an appeal. He went on to say that an appeal did not fall into the realm of the exceptions to the Hague Convention and that any further court proceedings should take place in the U.S. Did you get that? America, man! You three are heading home, my friend!"

Shmuel took the phone. "Scott, there is a bit more. I agreed to have you cancel any criminal proceedings you may have pending in the U.S. courts against Liza for kidnapping the children. I had to agree to this if we were to achieve our goal of getting the three of you home now. I also agreed that you would furnish an airline ticket for Liza if she wanted to continue this matter in the Milwaukee courts."

"You've got to be kidding me! I don't like this at all. She's completely messed up our lives and is not going to jail? She must pay, Shmuel. How did this happen?"

"I understand how you feel. Let me explain my thought process to you. Look, Scott, once you are safe at home with your children and Meg, you will call Julie and have her cancel the criminal proceedings against Liza."

"Hell no, I'm..."

"Listen, Scott, after a few days you will open up the proceedings again and no law will have been broken. This is the way to proceed, in my opinion. I hope that you do move forward with this so that the children will not be able to come back to Israel until they are eighteen. Regarding the airline ticket, who here is going to make you pay for it? No one is, Scott."

Stunned by his brilliance, I replied, "Wow, Shmuel, you are really good!"

"Thank you, but there is more. Opposing counsel wants to appeal to the Supreme Court and has been given 48 hours to do so. Remembering our ultimate goal of getting you and the children back home, we made another deal, which assures us that the three of you will be able to leave tomorrow. The judge has already told Liza's attorneys that the higher court will not even entertain their request and they know this, but they could keep you here longer by trying to appeal. Liza will drop any further attempts to keep the children here if you will forgive the money she owes you. In other words, all decisions by the appellate court will be followed and you are free to leave if you drop the $45,000 she owes you."

Remembering that Meg had said that Liza would never pay us what she owed, I most gladly, yet reluctantly, agreed to these terms. We would leave Israel on October 6, 1999, six arduous weeks after meeting David for the first time at the café in Tel Aviv.

We quickly packed our suitcases and checked out of the hotel. One hour later, we met at Shmuel's home outside the city. There, the three of us, along with David, Shmuel, and all of their children celebrated until midnight.

We ate and drank some scotch while going over last-minute preparations. We slept on Shmuel's couches for a few hours, but I barely closed my eyes from nerves and adrenaline. When I awoke, I began to reflect on the last six weeks and realized how quickly the courts moved our case along, although it seemed like an eternity for me. Shmuel asked, "Scott, is your job going to still be there for you when you arrive home? Six weeks is a long time to be away from work."

"You're correct," I muttered, exhausted. I contacted my manager and told him of the final outcome. He was pleased and simply wanted to know when I'd be home. I told him I'd be back in a few days. He told me to give him a call and he would get me up to speed on things.

David said, "I don't think you'll have much vacation time for the next few years, my boy."

I smiled thinking once again about all of the planes that flew over the beach in Tel Aviv and out to sea without us as I did my morning runs. Now we would be on one of those planes very soon, and I did not want to fly anywhere else once we landed in Chicago.

We said our goodbyes. It would be the last time I would see or speak to David and Shmuel. I needed to distance myself from my heroes because they brought back such painful memories.

For a guy usually full of things to say, I had few words to express my thanks. Sure, they were paid in full for a job well done, but they saved our lives. I was humbled and grateful for all of their emotional support during this hellish time. We climbed into the car for the final ride to Ben Gurion International Airport. The children were understandably sleepy, as these events weighed heavily on them as well. On our ride to the airport, both kids expressed their happiness to be going home, but wanted to talk to their mom. I promised that they could talk to her once we were checked in at the airport.

We entered the airport and I was cautiously optimistic as we approached the El Al ticket counter. I had called the day before to make the changes to the tickets. Things went smoothly as we were handed our boarding passes.

Still dragging, we made our way to the passport control line only to be asked to step aside upon reaching the podium. There seemed to be a problem with the children's passports. I feared we were in deep trouble.

We were quickly ushered into a room, and the kids wanted an explanation as to what was going on. "Dad, where are they taking us?" Ally asked, holding my right hand tightly.

"Guys," I said with a stern look. "I don't know what's going on. Let me find out and I'll let you know."

They listened as I answered all the questions thrown at me. The eye-to-eye contact was always intimidating to me, and I had border patrol and customs agents with guns watching me from three angles.

The three of us were left sitting at a table as the door shut.

"Um dad, I don't like this. Are we in trouble?" Jonathan asked. "I heard one of them say that you were not allowed to have us. Another one said that they might have to talk with you alone."

They both moved closer to my chair.

"Look, my loves, I will not let anything happen to you. We are fine. They just need to sort out some papers." I kept myself on high alert.

Finally, two border police walked into the room, leaving the door open. After almost an hour, a few phone calls, and almost soiling myself, they told me that they had cleared up the error.

Apparently, they had not received notice of the stay being canceled on the children's passports. My paperwork, along with whomever they called, satisfied everyone. Our papers were stamped and we were permitted through security. I recall holding my breath as we walked through, untouched, toward our gate.

As we walked I began to think about what had occurred in recent months. Emotionally, Meg and I had paid a heavy price to be with the children. Once again we were victorious in our quest to raise them and were able to, with excellent representation, get a foreign court to agree.

The children called Liza to say goodbye as we waited to board. I hurt for them as I saw the tears in their eyes and heard their somber voices, but I knew that they would certainly be better in time.

For likely the last time ever, I boarded an airplane leaving Israel for Chicago. Once again, I had my two very special reasons to be cheerful with me, though they were weary travelers at the moment.

Meg was amazed, surprised, and grateful at the outcome. She was also pleased with my decision to forget the money owed. As she put it, "Get out with the kids while you can." We were going to see each other in twelve hours, and it was going to be "one hell of a reunion for the four of us," as she put it.

As the plane headed west, my eyes filled with tears. Elated and tired, I could hardly believe that we three were heading home! I gazed at Yoni and Ally. They were listening to music and apparently comfortable enough to laugh and eat some of the food I had brought for us. I tapped each one on the hand and when they turned I whispered, "I love you."

They each smiled and said, "Love you too, Dad."

Once again I realized why I had fought so hard and had never given up. Meg and I believed in them and loved them dearly. We needed them in our lives, and like any animal protecting its young, we were willing to sacrifice a great deal to make it happen.

After the long flight we landed in Chicago, disembarked, and headed to customs. Meg had taken the day off work to come get us and stood waiting outside as we walked through Door B.

I needed to see her, smell her, and hug her big time, but I purposely moved slower to watch the kids' reaction. Each of them made a beeline toward her with smiles on their faces.

They embraced warmly, and then it was my turn. I warned them that this may take a few minutes. Meg said to me, "I missed you so much, sweetheart. I can't believe what you pulled off. I am proud of you and just want you to know that you will never be flying anywhere without me again."

"I can definitely live with that. I feel exactly the same way."

"Sweetheart, you performed fantastically in Israel under immense stress." Her words meant so much to me as the four of us headed to our car.

Our friends and family were overjoyed to know that we were back, and I must have told the same story a few dozen times. After two days of rest, both children appeared to be happy to be back in school and among their friends.

I contacted Julie to update her and she, too, was impressed at the outcome. We made arrangements to re-file our criminal charges against Liza and received a court date. One month later, the judge in Milwaukee listened to Julie and me in court and ordered that the children not go back to Israel until the age of eighteen. Liza did not attend the hearing, choosing instead to phone from Israel.

◆ ◆ ◆

EPILOGUE

◆◆◆

AS I WRITE this, it is December 15, 2012. The world is a different place than the day we landed in Chicago. Presidents have come and gone, we suffered through 9-11, and some tough wars, yet there were lots of good music and movies to keep our spirits up. The iPod was invented; iPhones are hot and computers became smaller, much smaller. The economy took a nosedive and many people have suffered, but things are looking a bit brighter.

Jonathan is twenty-five years old, graduated college and lives in Chicago. A smart and handsome kid, he is doing well. We talk often and I've even learned to text. Meg and I take the train down for visits when he can't come to Milwaukee. He has turned into a wonderful young man of whom Meg and I couldn't be more proud.

Ally is twenty-three years old, graduated college and lives in Milwaukee. We see her several times a month and talk often as well. She is a beautiful young lady with an abundance of talent.

She, too, has made us very proud. I guess you could say we dig them!

Meg continues to work in marketing and is doing well. She is quite talented and has only gotten better. I am impressed with most everything she does and love her dearly. We have been happily married for fourteen years.

Our wonderful dog, Jazz, is now thirteen and is the favorite of our neighborhood. We all love him a lot, too.

Both Jonathan and Alexandra have gone to visit Liza in Israel. Now that they're over eighteen Meg and I wanted them to choose where they would reside. Both chose America. They speak with their mother via Skype and cell phone from time to time. She has not let up on trying to convince them to move closer to her.

Both have often expressed how much they appreciate what Meg and I have done for them. We are grateful to hear these words and would do it again.

I don't speak to Liza. She has caused no further trouble for the four of us.

As for me, I am nearing twenty-eight years with Shaw Industries as a manufacturer's rep and have had a wonderful and successful career. I've come a long way from my days on the streets of New York selling Calvin Klein jeans. I am thinking about moving on soon to pursue writing and speaking full time.

THE END

FINAL THOUGHTS

◆◆◆

ACCORDING TO AMBER Alert Registry, a child goes missing every 40 seconds in the United States. That's over 2,100 per day. They go on to inform us that 800,000 children go missing every year and 90% are juveniles. 50% are 4-11 years old. Jonathan and Ally were as well.

According to NISMART-2 research from the Child Abduction Resource Center, which studied the year 1999, an estimated 797,500 children were reported missing; 58,200 children were abducted by nonfamily members; 115 children were the victims of long-term non-family abductions called "stereotypical kidnappings"; and 203,900 children were the victims of family abductions.

As in most of life's difficult moments, I was forced to learn a lot about myself.

I learned to fight for what I believe in realizing I just might reach my goal and become a bit wiser. This takes guts and a "never give up attitude". There were several times that I thought about giving up because the road ahead of me was simply too difficult. Yet, small steps forward gave me hope. Talking to others who were positive propelled me forward again and believing in what I was doing gave me the courage I would need. If I had not, my children would have grown up in Israel with a mother who surely would have hurt them psychologically. I cannot stress this enough. The moves you make, even if only by inches, help propel you forward. Do not quit. Giving up is not an option. Getting what you want is!

I learned to have fun and live life to the fullest. There were times when I was going through my own personal hell and I had to force myself to have some fun. I needed to detach from my misery and breathe. Life is precious and we must do our best enjoy it even when it appears that others are hung up in the daily grind.

I learned to say yes to silence when you are talking about the other parent with your kids. A parent who refuses to act like an adult during and after a divorce only hurts the ones they love. Saying yes to keeping quiet and not trashing the other parent is one of the finest things you can do for your children. Children grow and make up their own minds as to what occurred when they are better able to sift through the mess we parents created.

I learned that we are all the same in many ways. We need love and some luck. Continue to "check in" with yourself every day to see how you are really doing. Whatever obstacle(s) may cross your path, you can overcome them with hard work, sacrifice and once again, a bit of luck. I tried to be alert and proactive when life got in the way of living. This allowed me to live life on my own terms while giving myself greater control over many outcomes.

Sadly, I learned that as of December 2012, many of the 253 countries on our planet have not signed the Hague Treaty. You may be surprised at some of the names on the partial list that follows:

Afghanistan, Argentina, Armenia, Most countries in Africa, The Bahamas, Belize, Barbados, Bolivia, Cambodia, Columbia, Dominican Republic, El Salvador, Egypt, Fiji, Greenland, Gaza, Guatemala, Honduras, Iran, Iraq, India, Japan, Jamaica, Kazakhstan, Kuwait, Lebanon, Liechtenstein, Malaysia, Morocco, North & South Korea, Nepal, Nicaragua, Oman, Pakistan, Philippines, Singapore, Saudi Arabia, Syria, Thailand, Ukraine, Vietnam, West Bank, and sadly, many others.

◆ ◆ ◆

ACKNOWLEDGMENTS

◆ ◆ ◆

JONATHAN AND ALLY continue to be the lights in my life. Every day I am grateful for having the honor of raising them. Both have told me that I made the right move by fighting so hard to be with them. Both have thanked me for not giving up. I play their words back in my mind from time to time. I smile and maintain that I won the lottery the day I was awarded placement.

The three of us are better balanced, happier and quite lucky that Meg came into our lives. She immediately took on the role of step-mother, wife and helped to raise two wonderful kids. She continues to guide me, nurture me, love me and make me laugh every day. I try to do the same for her. She tells people that she's the lucky one and I feel the same way. Thank you for your support and insisting that I finish what I started. You never wavered and had many reason to do so.

This book came about because I had a story to tell. You might think it's rare that a man has his children kidnapped, but it isn't. Getting custody in the early 1990's was. I had a skilled attorney named Julie who helped me. Thank you, Julie. My attorneys in Israel were fantastic as well. David and Shmuel saved the day a second time! My heartfelt thanks to the two of you as well. Family and friends supported me even though they knew the chances of returning to America with my children were slim. My sincerest gratitude to each of you for never allowing me to throw in the towel.

Early readers/editors made *Kidjacked* better. They continued to polish my manuscript, breaking it down and building it up again and again. They made it shine. I send you my deepest thanks for your keen eyes and straightforward critique. It's what a writer really needs.

Laura, Tracy, Sandy, Bob, Meg, Lynn, Susan, Orit, Diana, Seth, Barbie, Janice, Shelly, Lori, Stacey, Christina and Luciana were so helpful in polishing the original 300 plus pages of material while providing much needed encouragement.

My senior editor Mike Sirota broke it down and helped me rebuild *Kidjacked* yet again with his expert vision, attention to detail and years of experience. Thank you, Mike.

◆ ◆ ◆

Recently, after speaking to a group, I was asked if I'd do the same thing again not knowing of the pain endured or the final outcome. I answered the only way I knew how.

"I never give up. I keep moving forward. That's how I got Jonathan and Ally home. That's how I was able to write this book. So, my answer is a resounding *yep!*"

◆ ◆ ◆